"The Death of Black Radio"

"The Death of Black Radio"

'The Story of America's Black Radio Personalities'

'A Personal Perspective'

Bernie Hayes

iUniverse, Inc.

New York Lincoln Shanghai

"The Death of Black Radio"
'The Story of America's Black Radio Personalities'

Copyright © 2005 by Bernie Hayes

iUniverse books may be ordered through booksellers or by contacting:

iUniverse
2021 Pine Lake Road, Suite 100
Lincoln, NE 68512
www.iuniverse.com
1-800-Authors (1-800-288-4677)

© 1997 U.V. Ltd.
© 2003 Bernie Hayes
© 2004 Bernie Hayes
© 2005-Bernie Hayes

ISBN-13: 978-0-595-35463-4 (pbk)
ISBN-13: 978-0-595-79956-5 (ebk)
ISBN-10: 0-595-35463-7 (pbk)
ISBN-10: 0-595-79956-6 (ebk)

Printed in the United States of America

The Aspiration!

My purpose in writing this book is to provide a useful reference and history for radio enthusiasts and the general public who are unfamiliar with the troubles and hardships of those pioneers who played a major part in the development, growth and culture of the broadcast and recording industries. I also wanted to offer a different medium for communicating with music lovers and aspiring performers. Investigation and exploration consistently demonstrates the strong influence African American announcers, male and female, contributed to the natural extension of oral or written information and cultural programming. They were proficient in supplying important and valuable messages. This book was written to make everyone aware of behind the scene activities, and inform the general public that there are alternatives. Community response can help make the industries honest, truthful and responsible. The industry should face the challenges of diversity in this new millennium. I wanted to examine the honesty of American culture. I have often wondered what would become of a society that seemed to have lost its culture of integrity, while ignoring key issues in media responsibility.

The use of self-censorship by early African American personality announcers was a strategy for cultural and economic survival. Black radio that had been considered primitive and unsophisticated, and black music that had been considered a harmful influence on the greater society, ultimately found recognition and acknowledgement as an ethical, articulate and informative communication style.

Repression and political persecution was a way of life for African Americans in the early part of the 20th Century. Observance of human rights in the North as well as in the South has not improved much for people of color. On the contrary some local governments have intensified repression. And because I grew up in a poor family, seeing and living in near poverty, I noticed very early the impact that media had on democracy and the American public. So my story is a personal journey through the dehumanization of particular classes and individuals, through the media, and the lack of opportunities that were available to members of my race.

I noticed that people needed hope, and the elders and adults in my community depended on information to improve their conditions, and they sought that information from the radio and Black newspapers. The information helped the people to obtain food, cloths and shelter.

The nation was bombarded with negative images, degrading cartoons depicting Black people as Sambo's and Coons, and propaganda filled with negative stereotypes that influenced group opinions. Undoing this damage is a very complicated issue and the people in the community needed to show the world that minorities were not only cooks, waiters, villains and victims, but people of worth.

Africa is the original home of humankind, and the cradle of intellect. Blacks were inventors, writers, architects, physicians, musicians, chemists, engineers and every other profession and vocation. But most of this information is kept from the general public. People are unaware of the three African Popes and it is not known that Black and Asian people first came to the North East in Roman times or that England was once ruled by a Libyan? Most facts such as these are hidden and omitted.

Hope came in the form of information. People needed to be shown that despite all of the awful things that were happening to them, there was an incredible amount of decency in the country and that information came from the Black radio pioneers and the Black Newspapers. I feel it is important to share with people who shared these same experiences and to enlighten those who did not and are unaware.

My parents and family, and our neighbors and friends relied on the *Chicago Defender*, the nation's most influential black weekly newspaper when I was growing up. The *Defender* reported on lynching, rapes, assaults, and other mayhem affecting black Americans. African Americans were referred to as 'The Race' and black men and women as 'Race men and Race women'. My community could not wait until they got a copy of the Defender.

Also, the *Afro-American* and the *Pittsburgh Courier* newspapers were favorites among my elders and others in the neighborhood. The Pittsburgh Courier was once the country's most extensively distributed black newspaper with a national circulation of almost 200,000. All of these publications helped us sustain cultural identity and racial pride.

The media in the early days portrayed African American families as dysfunctional and violent. I want this account to better expose the way it really was. Racism and the lack of information had a devastating social and economic impact on the way the nation and the world looked upon African Americans. Most people thought that entertainment, riches, power, pleasure, fame, or knowledge were the most important pursuits of people of African ancestry, but they were wrong. Freedom was first and primary. The additional was necessary but less significant.

CHAPTER 1

The Long Journey Begins!

My parents moved to Chicago from Jacksonville, Florida in the early 1920's, as part of the Great Negro Migration, when blacks were looking for jobs, educational opportunities and income in the North, and leaving the extreme racist sentiments and actions of white southerners behind, or so they thought. I never knew why they relocated to Jacksonville. It was never told to me.

Jacksonville has a very rich and glorious history of Black people. In the early part of the 20th Century, many black Africans escaping from slavery in the Carolinas and Georgia went to Florida and formed a union with the Seminoles. They became known as Black Seminoles.

A Black pioneer was named Abraham Lincoln Lewis. He founded Florida's oldest African-American insurance company, Afro-American Life in 1901, and the Lincoln Golf and Country Club. He started Florida's first black-owned and operated bottling company and aided and supported Booker T. Washington in founding the national Negro Business League, while providing financial support to Bethune Cookman College and Edward Waters College. Despite these contributions by some African Americans to businesses and to our culture, Jacksonville was however another southern city in segregated America.

Thousands of African-Americans moved from the rural South into the urban North. The resettlement of African-Americans changed the financial, social, and political structure both north and south of the Mason-Dixon line. That's the imaginary boundary named for surveyors Charles Mason and Jeremiah Dixon. The Mason-Dixon line was actually drawn about 100 years before the Civil War, but the borderline took on the role of a boundary in the war on slavery.

African-Americans began to play a role in the election of northern political leaders, such as Congressman William L. Dawson who in 1942 successfully ran for Congress and Adam Clayton Powell who became a member of the Seventy-ninth Congress on January 3, 1945. The Cotton Belt or the Promised Land would never be the same.

My mother, Alberta Missouri Burns, a beautician, was born in 1895 at Huntsville, Alabama. Huntsville is the heart of an area called the Black Belt because of its rich, dark soil and red clay. The constitutional convention was held in a Huntsville that paved the way for Alabama to become a state in 1819. My grandparents are buried in an ancestral cemetery at Redstone Arsenal in Huntsville. The family earlier in the century owned most of the land that the agency occupies.

My mother passed in 1954, and is buried in Burr Oak Cemetery. My father passed in January 1942. Both of my parents are buried in Burr Oak Cemetery in Alsip, Illinois, which is located on Chicago's southwest end. It is the cemetery where Emmitt Till, and his mother Mamie Till-Mobley are buried. Dinah Washington, blues greats Willie Dixon and Otis Spann are also buried there.

My father John, a barber, was born in 1892 at Dothan, Alabama. Dothan was first called Poplar Head Spring. Indian traders met there before the arrival of the white and black settlers in the 1830's. Through a special election on November 10, 1885, Poplar Head community became Dothan, Alabama. The George Washington Carver Interpretive Center, the Alabama Agricultural Museum, and the Wiregrass Museum of Art are located in Dothan.

My parents' occupations are listed on my birth certificate but I never knew either to practice these lines of work. As far as I knew, my father, a veteran of World War I, was a laborer and my mother was a housewife. My father worked for the WPA, The Works Progress Administration. It was part of President Franklin D. Roosevelt's "The New Deal". The programs were designed to provide jobs for the unemployed. Persons on the WPA built highways and were hired to do building construction, housing demolition and rural rehabilitation.

My mother had a beautiful alto voice and I am sure if she had chosen, she could have been a professional singer. They met in Florida, and were married in 1930 at Jacksonville. I had an older sister, Annie, who was born in Huntsville, Alabama when my mother was married to her first husband, whose last name was Lanier.

Like other Black people in the South, they moved to Chicago, which was heralded as the Land of Hope and Dreams. They settled on the near South Side. My older brother John, Jr., was born in 1933 at 38th and Cottage Grove.

They returned to Florida where I was born in 1935. A couple of months later, they returned to Chicago. We lived at 33rd and South Parkway, now Dr. King Drive, where I was nurtured. We again moved a block away to the 3300 block of Calumet Avenue. It was certainly a working class neighborhood, but at this time, it was really a village, where everyone cared and looked out for their neighbors. This village really did raise the children.

It was typical urban living, near schools, church, transportation. Some of my neighbors were Sylvester 'Two Gun Pete' Washington who lived a few doors from us, and recording artists and comedy team of Butterbeans and Suzie, who lived across the street. On the next block was Maurice McGhee, a teacher and musician. He conducted the choir for Rev. Clarence Cobb's First Church of Deliverance, and he helped write the score for the movie 'The Robe". On the same block were the Fitzgerald's, who were very politically connected. Congressman William L. Dawson was also a neighbor.

William Levi Dawson was born in 1886. Dawson became an alderman on the Chicago City Council, and in 1942 ran for Congress and won. He was the first African American to chair a regular House of Representatives committee. Dawson became one of Chicago's most dominant politicians, fulfilling his duty as an elected representative and a political power broker. He died in 1970.

Sylvester "Two Gun Pete" Washington commanded the Wabash Avenue police station, where people insisted he held Kangaroo courts for juveniles. In 18 years he claimed to have made 20,000 arrests and to have killed 16 men. He wore twin .357 magnums with pearl handles. He had a reputation as a rough, no nonsense officer who would not hesitate to use both of his pearl handled pistols on anyone he thought needed taming. In 1971 Sylvester "Two-Gun Pete" Washington, known as the deadliest cop in Chicago history, died at the age of 65 of natural causes. In the words of a fellow policeman, Washington "was the star of his own show."

Reverend Clarence Cobb was known as The Preacher, and help distinguish some of Americas top gospel singers and artists. He was one of the best-known preachers in the African American community around the nation.

In the area, we had the entire scope of typical neighborhood services, until the government implemented their urban renewal policies. The plan was supposedly to make the neighborhoods better, but it actually broke up the cohesiveness of the black family. Urban renewal is often referred to as Negro removal.

My brother and I attended Douglas Elementary School at 3200 S Calumet Avenue and we were members of Hartzell AME Church. The church that was located at 32nd and Prairie on Chicago's South Side was typical of Black Churches all over America. They were the cornerstones of the community.

Baptists, Methodists, Catholics, Pentecostals, all religions and denominations were part of our world. When social and community organizations were formed, most were created in the church. When issues tended to divide the Black community, they were usually resolved in the church.

After my fathers death the family moved to #50 west 35th Street, in 1943. My brother and I transferred from Douglas Elementary School to Keith Elementary at 34th and Dearborn. Keith was built in 1867, making it one of Chicago's oldest educational institutions. It was located across the street from the famous Mecca Building.

The Mecca Building was once described as "one of the most remarkable Negro slum exhibits in the world". The local media and historians wrote, "Perhaps no other building symbolized post-World War II urban decline more starkly than the Mecca Building".

The structure was built by the D.H. Burnham Company in 1891. The Mecca Building was considered a groundbreaking architectural model for luxury apartment living. It had courtyards, and skylights, fountains and flower gardens. The Illinois Institute of Technology (I.I.T) bought it and documents show that IIT had originally planned to raze the Mecca Building in 1941, but a tenants' protest had delayed the action. In 1950, tenants once again protested eviction by filing petitions with city and state officials, but it was finally demolished in 1952.

IIT was formerly the Armour Institute of Technology until 1940. IIT displaced a lot of neighborhood people from 33rd Street to 35th Street, and eventually bought nearly all of the property on State Street, Wabash and Michigan Avenues. It was urban renewal or 'Negro Removal' before the governments and local plans of the late 50's and early 60's.

CHAPTER 2

The Visualization!

I had always dreamed of a career in broadcasting. While a young child growing up on Chicago's South Side, I admired and envied such radio pioneers as Jack L. Cooper and Bob Roberts. Cooper was the nations first African-American announcer, although some might believe that the distinction belongs to Al Jarvis in California.

Before these pioneers, Black people could only listen to local white stations and some of the network shows that were broadcast. Most listened to Major Bowes and His Original Amateur Hour; The Jack Benny Program; Fred Allen Show; Fibber, McGee and Molly; Jack Armstrong—the All-American Boy and naturally Amos N Andy'.

Jack L. Cooper and Roberts, his brother-in-law, established Black radio in Chicago, over radio station WEDC. Emil Denemark Cadillac owned the station, where the call letter WEDC originated. The facility shared the frequency with foreign language and Negro programming. Cooper's radio show, "The All Negro Hour", debuted November 3, 1929 on WSBC, Chicago. Cooper stayed on the air in one form or another until 1961. He died Jan. 12, 1970.

WJTL in Atlanta presented a daily 15-minute newscast about the black community and delivered by black announcers in 1935.

Al Benson, Holmes "Daddio" Daylie and Sid McCoy came along soon after. 'Jockey' Jack Gibson and Oscar Brown, Jr., also developed a program on WGN entitled 'Destination Freedom' a Black radio series written by Richard Durham.

Daddy-O was as a bartender in the Beige room of the Pershing hotel and was convinced to go radio school and in 1948 he began Daddy-O's Jazz Patio on station WAIT. He and Mike Rapchak had the airwave humming at the time. Later he moved over to WMAQ radio and then 'The Voice for Equality' WAAF 950 AM. Daddio died February 6th, 2003 in Chicago.

Near the beginning days of radio, there was a mixture of encouraging and destructive stereotypes of African Americans. Most black characters were portrayed and represented as happy-go-lucky, ignorant, mumbling and incompetent, but in their communities, most African American announcers reached the status of icon, and a model of the community, but the story is usually partial, imperfect and somewhat legendary. A fact compounded by racism and mis-education.

All around the nation, African American personalities were entertaining and enlightening their audience with information and education. Some were very big in their respective cities and towns.

J.C.Marion, in his book "*Historic R & B Radio Moments*", chronicles some of the nations first and leading African American personalities. Some of the nations most talented personalities never achieved national recognition, nor were they nominated for induction into the Black Radio Hall of Fame, but they led the way, and opened doors for us to follow.

To demonstrate the diversity of black talent, you must remember the way America treated its black citizens and other people of color. Yet, some white owners opened their doors and some opened their hearts to African Americans. Some did it because they knew there was an untapped black audience, intact, and that meant more income for their facilities. Others recognized that times had to change, and progress was unavoidable and predictable.

In 1948, Gene Autry's hired Joe Adams (The Mayor of Melody), to work at radio station KOWL in Santa Monica, in order to tap into the Black community of Los Angeles. Adams appeared in the 1954 movie Carmen Jones, starring Dorothy Dandridge and Harry Bellefonte and more than 25 other films. Adams later became personal manager and road manager for the renowned Ray Charles, one of the most successful vocalist and musicians in the world.

In 1949 New Orleans station WMRY went to all black programming, and WDIA in Memphis obtained an all black announcing staff.

Oct. 25, 1948, Nat D. Williams made history by becoming the first Black radio disc jockey in the South on Memphis station WDIA. Nat was more than a mere disc jockey. He obtained degrees from Northwestern and Columbia Universities. He edited the "New York State Contender" newspaper and held editorial positions on the "Memphis World" and the "Memphis Tri-State Defender" and taught at Booker T. Washington High School. Nat paved the way for Martha Jean "The Queen" Steinberg, A.C. Williams and Rufus Thomas, all who became personalities at WDIA.

Another one of the early personalities on WDIA included BB King, whose real name is Riley B. King of Itta Bena, Mississippi, just a few miles from Indianola, and the hometown of Pervis Spann. He and I share the same birthday, September 16. In 1949, B.B had a radio show on WDIA radio show and a recorded a record for the Bullet Record Company. His nickname was the "Beale Street Blues Boy," but that eventually was abbreviated to BB. In 1951 he had a hit with "Three O' Clock Blues" and he went on to become a music legend.

B.B. KING

Direction
SHAW ARTISTS CORPORATION
565 Fifth Avenue
New York 17, New York

Rufus 'Bear Cat' Thomas was a singer while he attended Booker T. Washington High School in Memphis. In his early years, he began to write songs and got his recording career underway. Rufus formed a show business act with Robert Counce, and called themselves "Rufus and Bones". He later was one of Stax Records biggest hits, both as a solo and with his daughter Carla.

Thomas replaced BB King as a disc jockey at WDIA in Memphis. He died on December 15th, 2001.

Martha Jean *"The Queen"* Steinberg joined WDIA in 1954 and became one of the city's best-loved personalities. She later moved on to Detroit In 1982 and became a minister and a living legend there also; but Memphis will never forget Their Queen. She passed away in Detroit January 2000.

One more one of the earliest notable personalities was Maurice 'Hot Rod' Hulbert, who also began at WDIA. He worked with BB and Rufus "The World's Oldest Teenager" Thomas. In 1951 'Hot Rod' became the first full-time black DJ on an all-white station when he was hired at WITH in Baltimore. He later worked in Philadelphia and New York but finally returned to Baltimore. In 1964 he started at WWIN with Rockin' Robin, 'Long Lean' Larry Dean, Sir Johnny O and Al Jefferson. Hot Rod was enshrined in the National Rock n' Roll Hall of Fame in Cleveland. He joined our ancestors December 24, 1996.

In 1950 Willa Moore, on WDIA, was the station's first female African-American disc jockey, and the first black woman in the nation to host a radio program. She hosted a women's show focusing on homemaking, and advice to women. In the same year, former blues singer Reverend Dwight "Gatemouth" Moore became the stations and the nations first gospel disc jockey. The program was called 'Prayer Time'. Theo 'Bless My Bones" Wade also had a gospel show around this time.

During the 1950's many other cities began broadcasting to African Americans. WDAS and WHAT in Philadelphia; Detroit's WWJ; WLEY-FM and WBKB-TV in Chicago; WLIB in New York; WAAA in Winston-Salem, North Carolina; WEDR in Birmingham, Alabama; WMRY in New Orleans and WLIB in New York.

After learning that Memphis had a successful all-black station, Alex Leech and his brother, William E. Leech, opened the city's first black radio station, WJAK In Jackson, Mississippi, in 1954.

The first Black owned radio was WERD in Atlanta 1949. Jack "Jockey Jack" Gibson was one of the stations first personalities. He was the force behind NARA, the National Association of Radio Announcers, the nations first unification for Blacks in radio. He also published 'Jack the Rapper', the first trade magazine for Black music. In 1977 he started the Rappers music convention. I presented the first Dave Dixon award at the conference.

After retiring from radio, Gibson became the national promotional director for Motown Records and later for Stax Records.

Another one of the WERD personalities was Shelley "The Playboy" Stewart who began his radio show in August 1949. Shelly was a favorite with all ages and races.

In 1951 Mutual Broadcasting System presented the first all Black network radio program. MBS started as the Quality Network in 1929 with stations WOR New York, WLS, Chicago WLW, Cincinnati WXYZ, and Detroit. In 1934, WGN replaced WLS. By 1952, it had 560 stations. In 1972, Mutual launched The Mutual Black Network intended for black audiences and that later became the Sheridan Network. In 1973, Mutual Black Network and Sheridan Broadcasting Corporation combined, inaugurating the National Black Network

While a youthful adolescent student at Douglas and Keith Elementary Schools, on cold, wintry mornings, I would lie in bed listening to the radio, imagining the fun these personalities were having sitting in a warm studio, while they sent my elders and neighbors off to work to various occupations. Some of the neighbors were professionals and others laborers and day workers. We had a fair number of domestics, both male and female. I shuddered at the thought of getting up every morning, proceeding to some drudging, probably demeaning and low paying vocation. That is when I decided on a career in broadcasting.

These were my formative years. The time when my friends and I were thoroughly indoctrinated and brainwashed, thinking that white culture was better than what little Black culture we were exposed to even though *Ebony* magazine published its first issue on November 1, 1945. At that time we were not interested in reading magazines, not knowing we would have been so much more enriched in our culture if we had.

My friends, M.C. (Mack McClom), Junebug (Bernard Bush), Jesse James (Jesse Williams), Eddie (Eddie Bowie), Sam (Samuel Wright) and Paul (Paul Robinson) and I were taught the Columbus myth, and introduced to 'Tarzan, the King of the Jungle.' Tarzan was a young boy who was supposedly raised by apes and he was able to talk to the animals. He lived in trees and kept the 'uncivilized savage jungle inhabitants' in fear. We cheered for Tarzan, and when we saw the 'natives', we laughed and covered or faces with our hands, and made fun of those beautiful Black images on the screen. We considered them inferior and savage. We were well on our way of hating or ancestors, our elders and ourselves.

The lies fed to us about Columbus discovering America were never challenged. We believed what we were told, and the false and misleading images we saw in out textbooks. We did not know that his voyage of 1492 made him a murderer and colonist. We did not know that he was lost and in denial, and who never abandoned the belief that he had reached Asia. Columbus stumbled upon the islands he thought to be the Indies, and which have ever since been called the West Indies. He set foot on the Canary Islands, the Bahamas and Cuba, but never set foot on this land we live in called America. He massacred the indigenous people who befriended him and double-crossed people who trusted him. And this is the man our teachers and civic leaders has us calling a hero.

We had four movie theaters in my neighborhood. The States at 35th and State Street, The Louis that was named for Joe Louis at 35th and Michigan, The Terrace located at 31st and Indiana and The Grand at 31st and State Street. Once in a while we would visit The Owl at 47th and State Street, and occasionally The Tivoli on 63rd and Cottage Grove or the NRA at 58th and Indiana Avenue.

My friends and I had white heroes, such as Tim Holt, who played western heroes in many B-movies; from 1941-52 he was a top ten box office star; Tim McCoy, one of the earliest most popular western stars that always dressed in black, with a big white Stetson hat and a pearl-handled gun; Johnny Mack Brown, was from my father's home town of Dothan, Alabama. He was an All-American running back on the University of Alabama football team, and began doing bit parts around 1927 in silent movies; Charles Starrett was another one of the most popular of all cowboy stars, best known for his portrayal of the Durango Kid; Don 'Red' Barry, who was short and stocky, which a lot of us related to; Wild Bill Elliott, from 1940-54 starred in dozens of westerns of the '40s and early '50s, including many of the "Red Ryder" series and as Wild Bill Hickock; Tex Ritter, he co-starred with Bill Elliott and Johnny Mack Brown and later became one of the 'singing cowboys' we all wanted to be; Hopalong Cassidy, Sunset Carson, he wore his guns backwards like "Wild Bill", and boy was this guy cool, so we thought, not knowing he was of the ilk that was killing my people; Buster Crabbe who played "Flash Gordon" and "Buck Rogers" serials and as 'Billy the Kid' in western series; Buck Jones; Hoot Gibson; Lash Larue, he was known as the 'King of the Bullwhip'; Rocky Lane, and the other *singing cowboys,* Roy Rogers and Gene Autry. Randolph Scott and John Wayne were also stars of the silver screen but they were not as popular with my crowd as the others.

There were many others, really too many to mention. My friends and I had no idea there were African-American cowboys and cowgirls. I did not know of the many achievements and exploits of my people. We had no idea the first settler of the city I was living in was a Black man, Jean Point Baptiste DuSable. Nor did we know that O.T. Jackson, a Black man, founded Deerfield, Colorado.

We did not know of the Buffalo Soldiers that help settle the West; of the 180,000 African-Americans that served in the Union Army during the Civil

War, more than 33,000 died. Later the 9th and 10th Cavalries were nicknamed Buffalo Soldiers by the Cheyenne and Comanche. They made up 20 percent of all cavalry forces on the American frontier. The Black cowboys were left out of the books and off of the movie screen. We did not know that they worked on the ranches herding and branding cattle. They rode the trails and were at home on the plains. In fact, most of the real cowboys were black. We did not see or hear about the escapades of Bill Pickett, a famous cowboy from Texas, who was of black and Indian descent. He invented the sport of Bulldogging. Isom Dart, a real outlaw, was a black cowboy born 1855 in Texas. Isom drove herds on the trails and eventually settled in Brown's Park in extreme northwestern Colorado. Brown's Park was along the outlaw trail and was frequented by Butch Cassidy as well as others on the run.

Nate Love, also know as Deadwood Dick, a former slave from Tennessee; George Bonga, Dred Scott or Henry O. Flipper, who In 1877 he became the first African-American to graduate from the U.S. Military Academy at West Point. He served as an officer with the 10th Cavalry.

I was infused with lies and folk tales, fabrications, falsehoods and fables, all glorifying white heroes, while ridiculing and mocking my own people. This is the Chicago I developed in. The 'Promised Land.' This was the city that we thought reflected emancipation and liberty for Black people. To us it was 'the land of the free'.

We did have a few heroes and heroines that we could emulate. Heavyweight Boxing Champion Joe Louis, Olympic Champions Jesse Owens and Ralph Metcalfe, Mrs. Mary McLeod Bethune and occasionally Bill 'Bojangles' Robinson. Bojangles, when in Chicago would be in the neighborhood visiting a local tavern.

The Louis Theater as I mentioned earlier was named for Joe Louis. A picture of him in his fighting stance was in the lobby as you entered. Louis was from Alabama, as were my parents, so I connected with him immediately, feeling a sense of kinship because of our families' common roots. He was heavyweight champion of the world from 1937 to 1949. Joe was a symbol of pride for all black citizens and presented a glimmer of hope for all who wanted to achieve distinction and importance in the big, white world.

While he served in the Army during World War II, in class at Douglas Elementary School, the entire 3rd grade class had to recite out loud his quotation that said 'We will win because we are on God's side'. He changed attitudes among us and gave us confidence. We wanted to be like Joe.

Jesse Owens was also born in Alabama. In the 1936 Olympics, known as the "Hitler Olympics", Jesse won the 100-meter dash, the 200-meter dash and the broad jump, and was a member of the 400-meter relay team that won the Gold

Medal. Jesse was the first American in the history of Olympic Track and Field to win four gold medals in a single Olympics. Jesse overcame segregation, racism and bigotry. In 1976, President Gerald R. Ford awarded him with the Medal of Freedom.

Ralph Metcalfe was born in Atlanta, Georgia. He attended Marquette University in Milwaukee, and in the early 1930s, Ralph Metcalfe was the prime U.S. sprinter, winning most of the national titles. He competed in both the 1932 and 1936 Olympics. He won a gold medal, two silvers and a bronze. In 1936, he was second to Jesse Owens in the 100, and received a gold medal in the 4 x 100 relay. He tied the world 100-meter record of 10.3 eight times and the world 200 record once. When I was coming up he and Owens were successful businessmen in Chicago, and I would see them all over the Southside and eventually became friends with both.

Mary McLeod Bethune was a heroine to my mother and sister as well as every other woman of color that we knew. She was the representation of freedom for our people. Her parents were former slaves. She once taught school in Chicago and she would visit prisoners in jail.

She opened the Daytona Normal and Industrial Institute for Negro Girls in 1904, but later accepted boys. Because there was opposition from many at that time to educating black children, she attacked segregation and inequality facing African Americans. She said "Invest in the human soul. Who knows, it might be a diamond in the rough."

Bethune also opened a high school and a hospital for blacks. In 1923, she managed the school's merger with the Cookman Institute, in so doing the Bethune-Cookman College came into being

She later became interested and involved with politics. She helped integrate The Red Cross, and her biography notes, "In 1917, she became president of the Florida Federation of Colored Women. In 1924, Bethune became president of the National Association of Colored Women, at that time the highest national office a black woman could aspire. And in 1935, she formed the National Council of Negro Women to take on the major national issues affecting blacks.

Bethune served as director of the National Youth Administration's Division of Negro Affairs, Vice-President of the NAACP and served on President Truman's Committee of Twelve for National Defense. She also continued working with many organizations, such as the National Urban League, the Association of American Colleges, and the League of Women Voters. She was the first black woman to serve as head of a federal agency.

Throughout this period, Al Benson (June 30, 1908–September 6, 1978) also known as 'The Old Swing master,' was the most popular and most celebrated of Chicago's DJ's, and eventually became the most powerful, with the most time on the air. He would come on the air saying "Good Afternoon, ladies and gentlemen, this is your old Swing master Al Benson bringing you 60 minutes of red hot, beat me down, swing tunes of the day, and that's for sure." Al was an ordained minister whose church bought airtime from local radio stations. His real name was Arthur Leaner from Jackson, Mississippi, who came to Chicago in 1923. He changed it because he did not want his congregation or others in the religious community to know that he was playing what was considered 'the Devils music'.

The so-called Black Elite laughed at Al because he did not sound the way 'upward bound' Negroes should sound. He would mis-pronounce words, and sometimes talk with a mouthful of food. He had most of the national sponsors and nearly all of the local businesses sponsoring his shows. Some were Coca-Cola, National Clothing Co, Italian Swiss Colony Wine, Pepsi-Cola, Canadian Ace Beer, Ward Baking Co and Pekin Cleaners. Al would advertise the cleaners by saying "*YOU CAN'T BE RECOGNIZED IF YOU ARE NOT PEKINIZED.*" In 1960 I became the announcer that introduced 'the swing master', a fact that I will describe later.

Occasionally, 'Skeetz' Van, a singer, entertainer and protégé of Benson and a record spinner in his own right, would sit in for Benson. He worked for Benson and not the radio station. 'Lucky' Cordell, an announcer and future station manager of WVON, was also a colleague and member of Benson's staff. Lucky formerly worked at WGES and at WGRY in Gary, Indiana. He was known as The Baron of Bounce". If a record company or an artist wanted their product played in Chicago, they had to go through Al Benson. He had the power to make or break a record, and in some instances, a record company.

Benson established the career of quite a few singers and musicians, and played a large part in the success of gospel singer and legend Mahalia Jackson, acclaimed America's greatest gospel singer.

Mahalia Jackson was born in New Orleans, Louisiana, on October 26, 1911 or 1912, and died of heart failure in Chicago on January 27, 1972. She became acquainted with the "Father of Gospel Music," composer Thomas A. Dorsey in 1929. He became her musical advisor and accompanist from 1937 to 1946. Her signature performance of "Precious Lord Take My Hand," composed by Dorsey, became one of the most requested songs in her growing repertoire. Her recording of "Move On Up A Little Higher" sold more than two million copies, which he wrote for Mahalia Jackson in 1937. Dr. Dorsey also wrote 'Peace in the Valley,' "In October of 1979, Dr. Dorsey was the first black elected to the Nashville Songwriters International Hall of Fame.

Al Benson *in the 40's and 50's* also presented the major stage shows in the city at the Regal Theater, which was located at 47th and South Parkway. The Regal first opened On February 24, 1928. Benson was at the time, the foremost promoter of R&B and blues shows in the area. The Regal was the showplace for these acts, and a perfect venue for the thousands who wanted to see their favorite recording stars and comedians. The world's finest black entertainers performed here. It seated more than 3,500 and some of the acts that were presented include The Orioles, The Clovers, Dinah Washington, The Will Mastin Trio featuring Sammy Davis Jr., Red Saunders Band, Redd Foxx, Moms Mabley, Pigmeat Markham, Slappy White, Willie Lewis, Dusty Fletcher and many more.

Sid McCoy was the most popular jazz authority and promoter at the time. He started at WGES and in 1951 moved to WENR. He got his start in a voice talent contest held by Al Benson. Sid was on Midnights at WGES, and mesmerized the city with his golden tones and suave delivery. He was a real work of art. Sid was also a veteran of the airwaves and had developed one of the most loyal followings in the country. All of the jazz performers, both male and female, needed and wanted Sid McCoy as their friend. He was one of the nations top jazz personalities, along with New York's Symphony Sid and others around the country. He also worked at WCFL and teamed up with Yvonne Daniels for a short period.

CHAPTER 3

Sweet Home Chicago

I graduated from **Wendell Phillips High School** on the city's South Side. The school was named for the abolitionist who was one of the leading figures in the American anti-slavery movement. The school was racially mixed in the early days but by 1920 the school had become Chicago's first predominately African-American high school. During this period, the school's winning basketball teams formed the nucleus of a group that later became the **Harlem Globetrotters**.

Numerous noteworthy individuals have attended Wendell Phillips and been inducted in their "Hall of Fame," including well-known alumni such as entertainers Nat "King" Cole Nat who became a very famous jazz pianist and singer. He was the first black man to have his own radio show and later his own T.V show, and also appeared in quite a few movies; Dinah Washington won an amateur contest at the Regal Theatre and became one of the nations best loved blues and jazz singers; Sam Cooke, while in his teens became a member of the famous Highway Q.C.'s, and in 1951 he became lead vocalist of the Soul Stirrers. In 1957, Sam released "You Send Me" which shot up the charts to become a number #1 record: John H. Johnson, publisher of EBONY and JET magazines, and Fashion Fair Cosmetics, Supreme Beauty Products; and George E. Johnson of Johnson Products, became the first minority-run business to be listed on the American Stock Exchange; Alonzo S. Parham, the first African-American to attend West Point. There were so many more businesspersons and show business notables.

Maudelle Brown Bousfield was my principal until she retired. Mrs. Bousfield was a native of St. Louis, Missouri, a graduate of Sumner High School, the first African-American high school west of the Mississippi, and for many years the only African-American high school in segregated St. Louis. She was a Phi Beta Kappa and the first black woman to graduate from the University of Illinois. She served as the 6th Supreme Basileus of Alpha Kappa Alpha Sorority from 1929-1931, and the principal of Wendell Phillips from 1939 to 1950. She was the first African-American principal of a Chicago public school and was an important civic leader. Mrs. Virginia Lewis replaced her as principal in 1950.

Phillips High School was also noted for its athletes. It dominated in football and track. Clyde "Buddy" Young was born in Chicago, January 5, 1926. At the University of Illinois, he tied Red Grange's school touchdown record and later, in 1947, signed with the New York Yankees of the All-America Football Conference. He was one of the first blacks to play pro football because of a private injunction by whites to keep blacks out of the pro ranks from 1934 to 1945.

I graduated with Ira Murchison, a track star, who in 1951 was Illinois highschool champion in the 100- and 220-yard dashes. In 1956 he ran the leadoff leg of the 4 X 100-metre relays for the United States at the Olympic games in Melbourne, Australia, and helped propel the U.S. team to a gold medal in a world-record time of 39.5 seconds and at one time was known as the fastest man in the world;

Another classmate, Dillard Harris, a scholar and track star later became a General in the U.S. Air Force and afterward an educator and administrator. The Dillard Harris Educational Center, located in Joliet Illinois, is named for him. He was on the championship relay team with Albert Pritchett, Willie Burks and Jim Golliday and Ira Murchison.

Another schoolmate was Willie Stevens, who was a national hurdles champion at Wendell Phillips and Tennessee State University and is listed in the All-Time US record holders for the 110 yard low and high hurdles; Leonard Sykes who was one of the fastest men on the track field and holder of many state track titles; Ned Lenoir and Booker Rice, who also were record holders in track and field; Clyde Phillips, John and Barry Batson, Jim Golliday all were internationally known athletes.

I was captain of the football and track teams, the Boys Service Club, The Spanish Club and Philips Hi-Y. Our main school rivals were Dunbar Trade School, DuSable, Tilden Technical High and Englewood High.

CHAPTER 4

Race Records and Race Radio in a Racist Society

My announcing career began in 1953 while serving with the U.S. Air force in Alaska. I played jazz, pop and Country and Western, which were then labeled Hillbilly. In the 40's and 50's music was segregated, as was the country. Jim Crow was the law of the South. Record companies had labeled African American recordings as "race records," and black artists were limited to working what was known as the "chitlin' circuit; clubs and venues that catered to "colored" artists and audiences. The recording companies realized there was money to be made selling music by black artists to black customers.

The term Race Records was a particular term given to the labels that recorded Negro talent. Record companies such as Vocalion, Columbia, Okeh, and Paramount wanted to tap into the market and soon began to market these special labels to African-Americans who could not hear the music they loved and wanted to hear. A new genre was born. Race records were such a hit that other record companies entered the marketplace. Bessie Smith was one of the biggest stars on these particular labels. The record companies began themselves to give African American artists' record deals and by the 50s, race labels became unnecessary, but blacks were segregated in the marketplace by placing their product on special R&B charts and keeping the records out of the mainstream.

These were the glory days of Black radio, when air personalities in the African American community were images of accomplishment and excellence.

The radio and record industry was experiencing major changes on almost a daily basis, and black music and its impact on black culture, and these businesses were spectacular and historic. Because of the influence, the white record companies immediately sought to rule, dominate and isolate the art forms. They wanted to control the wealth, growth and prestige, and they would let nothing stop them. Motown was the exception.

Savoy was one of the earliest labels to cater to the African American market. They recorded most of the jazz and gospel performers at the beginnings of their careers. Some were Charlie Parker, Coleman Hawkins, Dizzy Gillespie, Little Jimmy Scott, Donald Byrd, Milt Jackson and Lester Young.

Other recording giants of the industry who recorded Black artists were; Apollo; Modern from Los Angeles; Hy-Tone in Chicago; Mercury in Chicago; Roulette Records who owned Gee Records. They featured Frankie Lymon and the Teenagers, who had several monster hits, The Cleftones and The Regents, Dinah Washington and Sarah Vaughn; Atlantic Records, owned by Herb Abramson, Ahmet Ertegun and Jerry Wexler. They had a lot of the major artists at that time, such as The Drifters, Lavern Baker, Ruth Brown, Joe Turner, The Clovers, and Sticks McGhee; James Bracken, his wife Vivian Carter Bracken, and her brother Calvin Carter owned Vee-Jay. Vee-Jay was the first large independent record company to be owned by blacks. Vivian was a former DJ who had started at WGES but moved to WJOB in Gary, her hometown. She was one of the most popular and liked dj's and always had a smile.

Some of their artists were The Dells, Gene Chandler, The Dukays, Eddie Harris, Dee Clark, Jimmy Reed, The Spaniels, El Dorados, The Magnificents, and The Shepards, and their gospel artists were Staple Singers, The Caravans, Gospel Harmonettes the Original Five Blind Boys, The Harmonizing Four and the Swan Silvertones; Sue Records was owned by Juggy Murray and Bobby Robinson.

They started in 1957 in New York City, and had Ike and Tina Turner, Elmore James, Barbara George, Baby Washington, Jimmy McGrif, Ray Bryant, and Inez and Charlie Foxx; Sun Records began by Sam Phillips; Okeh Record was eventually operated by Carl Davis, who called on Curtis Mayfield, Jerry and Billy Butler to produce Major Lance, The Artistics, The Vibrations, Walter Jackson, Johnny 'Guitar' Watson, Larry Williams and the Opals'; Aladdin Records including Floyd Dixon, the Cookies', the Sharps', and Thurston Harris, Marvin and Johnny, the Five Keys, the Jivers, Gene and Eunice, and Shirley and Lee. Chess-Checker and Aristocrat Records, for whom I later worked, was owned by Leonard and Phil Chess, and in the 50s and 60s dominated the Rhythm and Blues market with artists like John Lee Hooker, Elmore James, Muddy Waters, Bo Didley, Chuck Berry, Fontella Bass, Howling Wolf, Willie Mabon and Little Walter; King Records, owned by Syd Nathan had a lot of the R&B groups, most notably Bill Doggett, Sonny Thompson, The Dominoes, The Swallows, The Platters, The 5 Royals, The Charms and others; Specialty Records had both R&B and gospel artists. On the label were The Pilgrim

Travers, the Soul Stirrers, The Swan Silvertones, Alex Branford, Brother Joe May, Sister Wynona Carr, the original Gospel Harmonettes, Little Richard, Lloyd Price, Fats Domino, and Guitar Slim; Kent Records had B.B. King & a few others. African American Don Robey out of Houston, Texas owned Peacock Records. He later acquired Duke Records, a label that was started in Memphis by James Mattias. Liberty Records also was a major player as well as Dot, Nashboro-Excello and Red Robin.

The musicians unions were just as biased as the record companies and venues. The music developed in a framework of segregation and racist attitudes throughout the music industry. Some affiliates of The American Federation of Musicians were as racist as the Knights of the Ku Klux Klan. In the early years, the AFM strictly enforced its policy of segregation.

The common feelings among blacks as regards to union practices was suspicion because they were excluded and segregated and given the worst jobs *IF* they worked at all. They were very seldom allowed to work the first class hotels or clubs, or even on radio stations. During the early days of radio, musicians were the turntable operators and they kept the logs.

The Chicago unions reveal just how prejudiced and unjust these federations were. The white bosses of the white unions were thoroughly against integration. The members of Local 10 were white, while Chicago's black musicians belonged to Local 208. They were separate organizations. James C. Petrillo ran the white local and he rejected efforts of Local 208 members to merge with Local 10.

Philadelphia's unions had a comparable story. Local #77, the white union, barred Negroes so in 1935, Local #274 was formed as a separate Black Local. In Buffalo, New York, the black musicians of local 533 were kept segregated from 1917 until 1969. In Los Angeles, Local #767, The Negro Musicians' Union, was chartered in 1920 but did not merge with the white Musicians' Local 47 until 1953.

Although racial bias and discrimination has been a long and established way of life in America, the term has an even more negative overtone in the recording and broadcasting business. In the early days of radio, African Americans were describe and illustrated by negative stereotypes, such as Sambo's and uninformed, mumbling, unskilled and incompetent. When you were supposed to be respected in a business that demanded such treatment, the radio personalities of the early years had to fight a second war. It was a campaign that requested dignity and nobility.

In 1956, I was hired as a Soul and Gospel disc jockey at KDBS-1410 AM in Alexandria, Louisiana. Located in Rapides Parish. Ervin Ward-Steinman and the Lazarone family operated the Dixie Broadcasting Company, that owned

KDBS. One tradition says the community was named for the daughter of settler Alexander Fulton; another says it was named for surveyor John Alexander.

Alexandria is located near the center of the state. It was a typical Southern city, with all of the charm associated with the South. It has a rich history and race relations were more cohesive than most southern towns of this era. African-American culture integrated into the white culture and race relations were generally excellent. The general stereotypes did not accentuate the daily lives of the residents, either black or white.

The central African American district centered on Lee Street, where there were several Black owned business, including the Black owned Hollins Hotel. Dr. James Hines was only one of several Black doctors in the town and there were three Black owned funeral homes.

Alexandria is the boyhood home of author and Harlem Renaissance poet, Arna Bontemps. His poem, "A Black Man Talks of Reaping" received a *Crisis* poetry prize in 1926. He also wrote essays, short stories, fiction, nonfiction and children's books. During this time period from, 1924 to 1931, he was a teacher in a private school, the Harlem Academy in New York City. He received professional training in librarianship at the Graduate School at the University of Chicago and served as the librarian at Fisk University in Nashville, Tennessee from 1943 to 1966. The family home is now a museum in Alexandria.

Alexandria was a wonderful city. I replaced George "Groovy Daddy" Truehart. I was known as 'Bernie the Bellboy.' At that time because all Black DJ's had to have nicknames or aliases. I hated leaving my son Glenn in Chicago, but I was encouraged by family members and friends to take the job in order to launch my career.

I was the only Black DJ in the area so naturally I had the status of prestige. While Blacks lived in every section of Alexandria and Pineville, Louisiana, the main residential and entertainment district in 1956 was Lee Street, and another section known as Sam Town. It was an all Black community a short distance from the main part of the city. I was invited to MC all of the Black shows and advertise for the local promoters. I often taped shows to replay on the air the following day. Artists such as Shirley and Lee, The Ravens, The Crows and other performers on the 'Chitlin Circuit.' There were several imitators out there also. Imitators copied acts such as The Royales, who later became The Midnighters, and anyone else who had a hit record. Most audiences did not know what these acts looked liked since their recordings were mostly on 45-rpm discs, with no pictures. The venues were usually small dance halls or 'juke joints', and sometimes meeting halls. However, everyone accepted these conditions and rejoiced in every performance.

Record companies sought out radio record spinners and gave them records they wanted played on the air. Each DJ picked his or her own personal choices. There was no station designated record 'play list', meaning the jocks had the flexibility and freedom to play the music of their choice, and what they considered best and most suitable for their fans and audiences. Today, program directors, music directors and efficiency experts choose and dictate what DJ's must play.

In the late morning hours, I played gospel music for four hours, and in the afternoon, for another three hours, I played the soul hits. The music was pure. The Gospel recordings were of the Five Blind Boys, Sister Rosetta Tharpe, The Harmonizing Four, Wings Over Jordan, Mahalia Jackson and others who were popular at the time. Soul artists consisted of the giants of the era. Chuck Berry, The Orioles, The Spaniels, The Dells, Willie Mae 'Big Mama' Thornton, Muddy Waters and James Brown had his first big hit, 'Please, Please, Please.' Several imitation acts came to Alexandria pretending to be James Brown, The Ravens, The Crows and other artists who had hit records. Each record company had representatives who promoted their product. They were known as promotion people although the industry hired more than ninety percent males. They were often refereed to as 'record pushers', although that is a very uncomplimentary and belittling term.

In Alexandria, I became good friends with a young saxophone player who was just discharged from the U.S. Air Force. His name was Jules Broussard. Jules began his career when he was only twelve years old, organizing bands and playing lead saxophone for audiences in and around Alexandria and Pineville. He traveled all over the world and finally settled in San Francisco and we got together again when I moved to the Bay Area.

Jules was always aware of the limitations that he faced had he stayed in Louisiana in the mid 50's. Racial discrimination was not only a tradition but also the law. And music was strictly directed to specific audiences. Jules is one of San Francisco's most talented and loved artists.

While at KDBS I became the first Negro in Central Louisiana to do newscasts. Because I did not have a regional accent, most listeners, both Black and white, thought I was a white person catering to the Negro population. That soon changed in the African-American community as I began to make personal appearances and sought a place to live. I left the station less than a year later to return to Chicago.

I rode back to Chicago with Marion Walter Jacobs, known as "Little Walter", and his band. His real first name was Marion. Walter was a Chess recording artist who had a big hit at the time called 'Juke.' He was from

Marksville, Louisiana, near Pineville and Alexandria. At one time, he was a member of the Muddy Waters band, and he played with Wolf, Elmore James and Willie Dixon. His work was the finest and he contributed to the structure and molding of the blues in the early 1950's. He set the standards, which were above the norm. He was simply the best. He first made his mark in 1947 in the Maxwell Street area on Chicago's West Side, and his singing style was unmistakable. He was destined for recognition and success.

We stopped in Memphis and visited with 'Little' Willie John. He was real popular at the time. From 1956 to 1961, Little Willie John had fourteen hits on the R&B charts including 'Fever', 'Sleep', and 'Talk To Me, Talk To Me'. We came through St. Louis on or way back to the Windy City. Soon after my return to Chicago, my daughter Cheryl was born. The next year, another son, Sheldon was born.

In 1959, I was the announcer for 'Duke' Baldwin at WNJR 1430 A M in Newark, New Jersey. Duke was a professional tap dancer and instructor with his offices in the Theresa Hotel in Harlem. I was rubbing shoulders with Sugar Ray Robinson, Count Basie, Duke Ellington and the like. Tommy Smalls was a famous DJ in New York and he pretty much took care of me. I often spent hours back stage at the Apollo with my former schoolmate Sam Cook, Redd Foxx, The Clovers, Ruth Brown, Joe Turner, Ella Fitzgerald and other celebrities of that era. Those were good times, in particular being in an environment that had the conception of independence and emancipation.

I was particularly impressed with Sugar Ray Robinson, whose real name was Walker Smith. He treated me as a real friend. He earned the nickname Sugar Ray when a newspaper reporter described him as 'sweet as sugar'. He was the world welterweight champion at this time and later he held the middleweight title five times. He has often been referred to as the best fighter in history.

I returned to Chicago in 1960 and began writing for the Bulletin Newspaper. That is the year another daughter, Loriann was born. *The Bulletin* was a local neighborhood paper owned by the Sagan Corporation that provided community and regional information. That's when I met and became good friends with a young up and coming comedian from St. Louis named Dick Gregory. Dick was a regular at Roberts Show Lounge, a popular nightspot on the city's South Side.

Herman Roberts owned Roberts Show Club, and featured entertainers such as Sammy Davis, Jr., Redd Foxx and Della Reese. He founded the first Roberts

Motel because entertainers at his club found it difficult to acquire accommodations in the city. He soon opened four others.

Alvin Cash of 'Twine Time' fame was auditioning as a dancer at Roberts Show Club at the time. We all became good friends. At the Bulletin I was entertainment editor and my mission included visiting radio stations and interviewing celebrities, including recording artists and other show business representatives and professionals.

This was at the height of the civil rights crusade, and Dick Gregory was an active participant in the movement. I accompanied him on several demonstrations around the area. The early years of the struggle were tumultuous and turbulent, but nothing compared to what was to occur a few years later.

Dick Gregory, was from St. Louis, and is now known as he was then, a comedian, but most of all, a civil rights activist. His performances changed the comic scene, and the way America appreciated and recognized African Americans.

A phenomenon among African-American people in the Forties and Fifties was the discrimination of different appetites of the masses. Some thought they were too cultivated to enjoy Rhythm and Blues music. Some deemed themselves as Jazz advocates and preferred to put down those who enjoyed R&B.

In 1961, I became the chief staff announcer at WGES, replacing the late Tony Ford. It was the major Black oriented radio station in the Chicago area. WGES began broadcasting in 1923 as WTAY. It became WGES in 1925 and began airing on 1390 in 1941. Doc Dyer sold the station in 1962, and the call letters were changed to WYNR. It is now WGCI. I will tell you more about this story later.

The air personalities at WGES were my idols. The Old Swing master-Al Benson, Sam Evans, Richard "Open the Door Richard" Stamz, Ric Ricardo, Norm Spaulding, McKie Fitzhugh and Sid McCoy. The cream of the Midwest' broadcasting talent. The station also featured foreign language personalities. Bill Fields, who had worked at the station a few years earlier, returned and joined me as a staff announcer.

One of my fondest memories was one early summer morning when I was at the station for a meeting, all of the personalities were there and it seemed like every record promotion in the city happened to visit the station that day. I remember everyone was so pleased to see Sid McCoy since he was the midnight personality and was seldom seen at the station. Granny White, George Williams, Ernie Leaner, Bunky Sheppard and all of the announcers and dee-jays had a wonderful time seeing one another. I was also the announcer for the 'Polish Early Birds', Amerigo Lupi and 'Madam Puchinska.' I also did a Sunday Jazz program.

Some young people visiting the station practically daily were up and coming artists Gene 'Duke of Earl' Chandler, who as a member of The Dukays, recorded "Nite Owl" and "Duke of Earl" in 1961; Major Lance, who went to high school with Curtis Mayfield. He was in a group called the Floats. Later he recorded "Delilah" and finally did his big hit on Okeh records for Carl Davis called "Monkey Time". He also had hits, all written by Curtis Mayfield called 'Hey Little Girl', 'Um Um Um Um Um Um', 'The Matador', 'Rhythm', and 'Ain't That A Shame'.

Dee Clark. Dee had a lot of hits around Chicago and the nation. Herb Kent gave him the break he needed and got him a recording contract. Some of his hits were 'Nobody But You', 'Hey Little Girl' and 'Just Keep It Up'.

Jerry Butler

On one occasion, Columbia Records promoter, Granville 'Granny' White and former Chess producer, who was now with Columbia, Ralph Bass, brought by a young up and coming female singer named Aretha Franklin. They had high hopes for this preacher's daughter from Detroit and they wanted her to meet the designers and movers of the music industry in Chicago. They introduced Aretha to all of the personalities and announcers. That was the custom. That is the way it was done. Each DJ was an independent businessman or businesswoman. They 'brokered', or purchased the airtime from the owners. Each programmed their own shows and obtained their own sponsors. They occasionally shared their earnings with the station owners depending on the agreement they had made with the owners.

Another frequent visitor to the station was a former high school classmate, Eddie Thomas, who was managing a young group of entertainers whose names were Jerry Butler, Curtis Mayfield, Sam Gooden and Fred Cash. They called themselves 'The Impressions.' Curtis taught himself to play the guitar. In 1957, he teamed up with Jerry Butler and the group was called The Roosters. Eddie Thomas renamed them The Impressions and became the group's manager. Their first hit was "For Your Precious Love" and the rest is history. He wrote songs such as "Gypsy Woman", "The Woman's Got Soul"," It's All Right" and "I Loved and I Lost. He and Eddie Thomas later started their own label called Curtom, a combination of their respective names. I became their distributor in St. Louis in 1965.

Pervis Spann, Franklin McCarthy and 'Big Bill' Hill, who were disc jockeys at Oak Park radio station WOPA, were frequent visitors to WGES also. Spann and Big Bill mostly played blues and were both promoters of ventures that mostly showcased blues artists.

Pervis Spann is known as "The Blues Man." Pervis was born in Itta Bena, Mississippi. Pervis became one of the foremost promoters of blues and R&B shows in the city and is now the current owner of Radio station WVON and several other stations around the country. Spann began managing entertainers and booking shows. He also owned several nightclubs

In 1975 Spann bought 1450, called it WXOL and in 1983 the WVON call letters were restored.

Big Bill Hill owned several businesses in Chicago including Big Bill Hill Dry Cleaners and the Big Bill Hill Nightclub. Most of the time his shows were live remotes with artists like Muddy Waters, John Lee Hooker, Little Walter and The Howling Wolf. At one time he was the king of blues radio in the Midwest.

Another constant visitor was Jerry 'Jerrio' Murray, who later made a record that was to become a national symbol called 'The Boogaloo.' by Tom and Jerrio

.In 1964 the record had the phrases, 'sock it to me' and 'let it all hang out,' and soon after, those phrases were heard all over America, and ultimately all over the world. Their next release was a single by Jerrio called "Karate Boogaloo". Jerrio later produced several records that I recorded for Stax Records.

Record promoters who visited the disc jockeys represented all of the major and independent labels at the time. Most were housed on '"music mile" or "record row" a section of Michigan Avenue between 14th street and 22nd street (Cermak Road)."

The leading record distributors were All-State Distributors, which had thirty-six labels including Smash (Mercury), Motown, Stax, and Brunswick. King Records was also on Record Row. M-S Distributors, Garmisa Distributors, Columbia Records, Capitol Records, RCA, Mercury, MGM, Vee Jay and Constellation Records, and later, Chess Records and recording studios moved to 2120 S. Michigan. It is now a museum, named after Willie Dixon.

United Record Distributors headed by Ernie Leaner, was the only Black owned distributor. African-Americans also owned Vee Jay Records and Constellation Records, as I illustrated earlier. Ernie's brother, George, ran their record company, Onederful Records. "Shake a Tail Feather" was released on Onederful Records.

Payola was not an issue among Black disc jockeys. Although some of them took money to play certain records, it was nothing compared to what the white disc jockeys were receiving. The practice was outlawed in 1960, after a number of disc jockeys were accused with taking pay offs from record companies to play their songs. In those days, a $100 bill could have a deejay 'lean' on a record, and $200 would get double the play.

The scandal broke wide open in the late 50's, but what Negro announcers were getting was a mere pittance to what whites were taking. On May 9, 1960, Alan Freed was indicted for accepting $2,500. Later, the government passed the anti-payola bill and the practice became a misdemeanor, with a penalty by up to $10,000 in fines and one year in prison.

The House Oversight Subcommittee was asked look into the recording industry's practice of payola. The committee decided to look into deejays that took gifts from record companies in return for playing their records on their shows. Fearing the worse the record companies began telling the committee the names of disc jockeys that they had given money to. Soon twenty-five dee-jays and program directors were named and that created a scandal. All were white, namely Joe Niagara of Philadelphia, Tom Clay of Detroit, Murray "The

K" Kaufman of New York and Stan Richards of Boston. The investigation then directed its attention Dick Clark and Alan Freed, formerly known as Moondog, the two top deejays in the country.

Clark revealed that he had a 27% interest in records played in the past two years and he had an investment in Jamie Records. Jamie records paid Clark $15,000 in payola, but Clark denied ever accepting any money. Alan Freed later was drummed out of the industry and died poor. Clark is still going stronger than ever.

Howard Bedno was the head of local promotions for All-State Distributors. Paul Glass ran the company, the largest of the independents. All State carried Motown, Gordy; Atlantic, Chess, Checker, Cadet, and Stax, while renowned record producers and promoters Ewart Abner and William 'Bunky' Sheppard essentially ran Vee Jay and Constellation Records. A customary stop for me after work at WGES was the record store on the West Side owned by Richard Stamz, or Batts Restaurant on 22nd Street near record row. At Stamz place you would find Bobby Rush, Otis Rush, Syl Johnson, Cicero Blake and other ambitious and aspiring singers and musicians getting together telling of their latest adventure or ordeal. It was like a family gathering every day.

WGES was sold in 1962 to the Gordon McClendon Group of Dallas, Texas. He and Todd Storz, then owner of WHB of Kansas City, were competing for the top 40 markets. After WGES was sold to McClendon, the sound of Chicago black and pop radio changed forever. Storz is the person most people will acknowledge who originated top 40-formatted radio.

The McClendon group brought in Jim Randolph from KGFJ in Los Angeles as Program Director. Randolph was the first Black program director in the history of Southern California radio. Randolph returned to KGFJ after leaving Chicago.

In 1962, another radio station opened in the Chicago area. WMPP in East Chicago Heights, Illinois received a license from the FCC to broadcast on 1470 AM. It was the first Black Owned radio station in the area. Chicago businessman William Martin and a small group of his constituents collaborated and formed Seaway Broadcasting Company, Incorporated. The owners acquired permission from the FCC to operate on Lincoln Highway and Ellis Avenue in the south suburban city. Jesse Coopwood of Gary, Indiana and I were the programmers who were responsible for formatting the facility and hiring the jocks.

The station quickly gained popularity and became a favorite with music lovers all over the area. It was only 1000 watts and the signal was limited to covering predominantly the Southeast area and was not very strong downtown or on the Westside. I left to join the staff at WVON.

1964

BERNIE HAYES

Disc Jockey - Music Authority

Jazz personality, disc-jockey and music authority at radio WMPP. Mr. Hayes is a newscaster, reporter and writer and was the first Negro to become a newsman in central Louisiana. A graduate of the University of Illinois; he has been in the broadcast medium over nine years, working as disc-jockey, staff announcer and writer-salesman.

Mr. Hayes has one of the best liked and discriminating deliveries of today's top-notch announcers; always striving to make the broadcasting industry conscious of the image of the "modern Negro". Hayes plays music to stimulate and to educate the radio listener.

Like the entire staff of Radio - WMPP Hayes is devoted to the entire Chicagoland area, and is dedicated to the principles on which WMPP was founded. That is, to making WMPP the best programmed and best sounding radio station—regardless of origin or ownership in the entire country.

Bernie Hayes is a dynamic part of the first Negro owned and operated radio station in the mid-west.

WMPP

Is The Negro Market

Most Black radio personalities had an exclusive and exceptional way of opening their programs. Rosko, E. Rodney Jones, Poppa Stoppa, Jack Gibson, Hot Rod Hulbert and Bugs Scruggs were just a few of hundreds of African American Deejays who kicked off their programs with singing rhyming jingles. All were quite innovative and unique and usually written by and performed by the jocks themselves. I began using this type of opening in 1964 at KSOL and continued the practice through the 70s.

CHAPTER 5

Black Personality Deejays becomes an endangered Species!

This is the period that I first noticed the life draining from Black Radio. The toll bells were ringing. Todd Storz owned stations in Omaha, New Orleans, Kansas City, Minneapolis, Miami, Oklahoma City and St. Louis. The call letters were changed from WGES to WYNR, known as *'the winner'*, and the format was changed from R&B to more of a Pop or white oriented station, playing only a smattering of Black artists. Jim Randolph, a former west coast DJ was named program director and Mike McClennan was named news director and the African-American legends were dismissed and replaced by young white announcers like Dick Biondi, Ed Meyers and Dick "Wild Child" Kemp. The blacks were Johnny Evans and Floyd Brown who were staff announcers and I was hired as a newscaster.

Bernard Shaw also started at **WYNR**. Shaw went on to an illustrious career in broadcasting, including Chicago stations WNUS, WFLD, and WIND. He later became a White House reporter for Westinghouse Broadcasting Company, CBS News, ABC, and a news anchor for CNN.

It would be a smooth changeover for the stations management, but to the previous staff and to the general public, it was shocking and devastating. The switch from rhythm and blues to a top 40-pop oriented format was another blow to the African American community and to the tens of thousands of white listeners who loved the R&B sound.

On September 1st, 1962, WYNR dj Dick "Wild Child" Kemp started at midnight, and until 1 a.m., the first day of the new format, and the music play list had changed overnight. African American artists were immediately relegated to second class, replaced by *Joanne Campbell—Girl from Wolverton Mountain; Joey Dee—Wingding; Bobby Vee—Punish Her; Frank Ifield—I Remember You; Neil Sedaka—Breaking Up Is Hard To Do; Four Seasons—*

Sherry:Elvis Presley—Tell Her Jim Said Hello—Wanderers—There is No Greater Love and Ventures—Lolita Ya Ya.

The Rivingtons—Papa Ooh Mow Mow Mow, The Marvelettes—Beechwood 4-5789, Gene McDaniels—Point of No Return, The Duprees—You Belong To Me and the Fiestas—Broken Heart were the only black artists on the list, and as the night progressed, the list became whiter. These records replaced Black artists who were on the R&B charts. For example, Unchain My Heart—Ray Charles; I Know (You Don't Love Me No More)—Barbara George; Duke Of Earl—Gene Chandler; Twistin' The Night Away—Sam Cooke; Soul Twist—King Curtis: Mashed Potato Time—Dee Dee Sharp; I Can't Stop Loving You—Ray Charles; You'll Lose A Good Thing—Barbara Lynn; The Loco-Motion—Little Eva; Green Onions—Booker T. & The MG's; You Beat Me To The Punch—Mary Wells; Do You Love Me—The Contours; Release Me—Esther Phillips and You Are My Sunshine—Ray Charles.

Bernie Hayes

It was a perfect time for another black oriented station. It would have been an ideal time for blacks to enter the market as owners. Doctors Bell and Cox in Detroit would have been just right to enter the Chicago marketplace. The challenge went unanswered therefore the Chess brothers benefited from the opportunity.

Yvonne Daniels, daughter of singer Billy Daniels, "The First Lady of Chicago Radio," was an African-American broadcast pioneer. E. Rodney Jones brought her to WVON and later she worked on almost all of the major music stations in Chicago. She began her radio career at WBBR in East St. Louis, Illinois. Later she joined WYNR and soon after she teamed up with Sid McCoy on WCFL.

Yvonne was an instant hit at the station. I was hired as a newscaster. I stayed at WYNR until early spring of 1963, when brothers Leonard and Phil Chess bought radio station WEDC and changed the call letters to WVON. They owned Chess and Checker Record Company. Artists on the labels consisted of Little Walter, Minnie Ripperton, Etta 'Peaches' James, Muddy Waters, Howling Wolf, Sugar Pie DeSanto, Mitty Collier, Bo Didley, Chuck Berry, Fontella Bass, 'Sonny Boy' Williamson and other Blues, Jazz and R&B legends and pioneers. They were legitimate trailblazers.

I worked as a salesman and DJ at the new station, and I recorded most of the on-air commercial announcements. The personalities included E. Rodney Jones, Pervis 'Blues Man' Spann, Herb 'Cool Gent' Kent, 'Lucky' Cordell, Bill "Doc" Lee and Ed "Nassau Daddy" Cook. Ric Ricardo was in the sales department also. Cordell and Lee had formerly worked with Larry Wynn on radio station WBEE, which was situated in Harvey, Illinois, a south suburb.

WVON solidly became number one in the market because of the music and the relationship the personalities developed with the community, and the award winning news department, under the directorship of the extraordinary newsperson and personality, Roy Wood. Jim Maloney was the other main newscaster, and I was also contributing news updates. Spann became the major promoter of R&B music shows in the city. He took over the bookings at the Regal Theater, succeeding Al Benson. I sat in for Rodney and Spann when they decided to take time off. Rodney and Pervis evolved into two of the most popular and wealthiest disc jockeys in Chicago. Lucky Cordell eventually became station manager. Rodney was the program and music director. E. Rodney Jones passed January 2, 2004.

Soon after the WGES sale, another giant appeared on the radio horizon. It was clear that **personality radio**, as we knew it, was nearly finished, although many didn't recognize the signs at that time.

Leonard Chess died in 1969 and the business was taken over by Phil and Leonard's son Marshall. In 1975, Joe and Sylvia Robinson bought the label and they sold 2120 South Michigan. Joe and Sylvia owned Sugar Hill Records, who started the rap music genre; Sylvia was best known as part of the singing duo Mickey and Sylvia who brought us "Love is Strange' and she as a solo artist with 'Pillow Talk". In 1969 most of the independents also were on the decline during this period. Most of them were out of business by the middle seventies.

I produced and promoted my first stage show in 1963, at DuSable High School. The acts were Walter Jackson, who was more of a crooner than a rhythm and blues singer. He disliked people calling him a R&B artist; The Chi-Lites, Eugene Record, Squirrel Lester, Creadel 'Red' Jones and Marshall Thompson; The Radiants, who consisted of my classmate Maurice McAllister, Leonard Caston and Wallace Simpson; Jackie Ross and a few other local artists who had hit records at the time. They did not charge me for their talents. They in fact did it for me.

The show was not a big success, but it did all right. From then on, I was hooked on developing shows and talent. In the spring of 1964, I left to accept a position as a disc jockey at KSOL, San Francisco.

CHAPTER 6

The West Coast Chapter!
Sojourning the Middle Passage!

I left Chicago for San Francisco in March of 1964. My cousin's husband, John Moutrey made the trip with me. We took the northern route. Our first stop was in St. Louis, Missouri, never suspecting that I would spend time here later. We saw what was to be The Gateway Arch, but at the time, it was just a construction site with two silver legs sticking out of the ground. Percy Green, the former head of ACTION, protesting the absence of minority workers building the Arch, climbed halfway up one leg of the structure before he was arrested.

Bernie Hayes on air at KSOL

The St. Louis Baseball Cardinals won the World Series in 1964, but I was a Chicago Cubs Fan. And the St. Louis Football Cardinals, who at one time was the Chicago Cardinals, had a pretty good season in 1964.

We spent only a few hours in St. Louis and drove to Kansas City, where we stopped on 12th and the Paseo to have a steak dinner. Denver was delightful, driving above the clouds and watching airplanes flying below us. That was an experience. On to Salt Lake City and the Mormon culture all around us. We the continued on to Reno, Sacramento and finally reaching the Golden Gate and Bay Area three days later. It was dusk when we saw the City. It was a marvelous sight. The locale was a sprawling metropolis, spanning both sides of the Bay. It was breathtaking.

This is the same area that I spent my basic training in the U. S. Air Force. In 1953, while studying at the United States Armed Forces Institute through the University of Illinois, I was stationed at Parks Air Force Base in Pleasanton, California, also in the San Francisco Bay Area. I was always attracted to the locale by the Rice-A-Roni commercials I had seen on television.

I finally settled down 211 Monroe Drive, on the boundaries of Mountain View, Palo Alto and Los Altos, near San Antonio Road and El Camino Real. The house sat at the intersection of all three municipalities.

The backyard was the size of a football field with several assortments of wild roses and lilies, and a variety of fruit trees. It was enchanting to a person who had grown up on Chicago's crowded and busy South Side. To me, it was a favorable change. Although the daily morning drive was approximately forty minutes on Highway 101, nevertheless it was pleasurable, even in the thirty-degree weather. I am sure you have heard about the weather in and around San Francisco.

I was hired at KSOL by Tom Johnson, the former production director at Chicago's WVON. He was contracted by the owners to overhaul the facility, which was formerly known as KSAN. The station, owned by Les Malloy and Del Courtney, wanted to be the owner of the names of all of their personalities, so I became ***BILL STEWART*** on the air. I did not want to change my name, but it was station policy.

KSOL was located in downtown San Francisco, at Seventh and Market Street. KSAN, at AM 1450khz had George Oxford, who eventually went over to KDIA in Oakland in early 1960, John Hardy, who joined George in 1961, and Rockin' Lucky.

Our main competition was KDIA, the other R&B station that was located across the Bay in Oakland. I was the morning DJ, holding down the 6:00 a.m. until Noon spot, and later, 6:00 a.m. until 2:00 p.m. Bob White, a Kansas City native, followed me from Noon until 4:00pm. He replaced Chuck 'Bugs' Scruggs who left us to accept a position at KDIA in Oakland. Herb Campbell took over at 4:00 p.m. and played until 7:00pm. We hired a young San Francisco musician to do the evening show. His name was Sylvester Stewart, but he eventually became famous as Sly Stone. Sly Stone's recording career began in 1948 with his family's group, the Stewart Four. Sly also later worked at KDIA. George Oxford also went over to KDIA in Oakland as well as John Hardy.

The chief engineer did the overnight slot. As a station policy, I and the other announcers had to change our names, because the station wanted to 'own' the personality spots. Chuck 'Bugs' Scruggs, who had worked in Cincinnati with Ed Cook and Jockey Jack Gibson, later became a major player in changing Memphis radio.

KSOL easily became the leading radio station for African-Americans in the region. I am delighted to say that I played a predominant portion of this distinction. I introduced new recordings and artists to the area that were practically unknown in the region. Tom and Jerrio's recording of Boogaloo became a smash hit on my morning show and eventually went on to become a national hit. Bobby Freeman along with Sly was making quite a name for himself also, and across the Bay, Joe Simon was kicking it up in Oakland.

Slim Jenkins nightclub on Seventh Street was the place to go in Oakland. In the early 50s and 60s Jenkins had the largest African American community in the Bay Area. Most social gatherings, and the majority of the black professionals and businesspersons had their offices along 7th Street. It was the central point of African American activity, and one of Oakland's first profit-making centers.

Oakland's KDIA had Chuck 'Bugs' Scruggs, the man with the plugs back on the scene with his record machine, was inducted into the Cincinnati Broadcasters Hall of Fame in 1992.' Scruggs, a veteran who was one of the original jocks at WCIN in Cincinnati, left KSOL to work at KDIA. He left Oakland to run a Memphis radio station and today hosts"ready to learn" children's show on public TV and radio in Memphis.

The pop radio stations were "Boss of the Bay, KYA", who played the Rolling Stones, the Byrds, Beau Brummels, Paul Revere and the Raiders, and other such groups. KSFO, KFRC, KNBR, KCBS, KGO (Talk), KEWB, KABL, KFAX, KYA. Some of the personalities were Don Sherwood, Dave McElhatton, Doug Pledger, Jim Dunbar, Gene Nelson and Van Amburg,

In the midst of the 1960s the Haight-Ashbury district was the center for San Francisco's rock bands and hippie and beatnik culture. It was the home of "The Grateful Dead" and others. The music industry was experiencing changes that would reverberate all through the land. It was at the same time the period of the British Invasion. The first band to make an impact was the Dave Clark Five, and then the explosive entrance of the Beatles, The Animals, The Moody Blues and many others.

These groups had a leading influence on American Rock and Roll, and nearly pushed Rhythm and Blues out of the market. American artists had to fight for a place on the charts and Black artists and radio stations were nearly completely overlooked and some disregarded. Racism was again raising its ugly head and creeping into the front offices of the major record companies. The majors controlled the distribution as well, therefore creating a disastrous and devastating position for African American artists and labels.

One of the most powerful record storeowners in the Bay Area was **Ray Dobard**, who owned Music City Records in Berkeley. He knew his way around the recording industry, and recognized the changes that were taking place. He understood that Black radio, as we knew it was about to go through a disturbing change. The days of independent record promotion and personality radio announcers faced trouble in the future. I agreed with him during the hundreds of conversations we had. Dobard owned a record company, and was a talented record producer, promoter and songwriter. He recorded some of the most popular groups in the Berkeley, Oakland and San Francisco area. The days of personality radio was already being transformed.

This was the height of the Civil Rights movement. Dr. Martin Luther King, Jr. and the S.C.L.C. were carrying on protests in the South along with SNCC and CORE, and several other alliances and students. The Freedom Riders had invaded Mississippi and Alabama. Stokely Carmichael, H. Rapp Brown, Ben Chavis, Dick Gregory, James Farmer and thousands more were protesting and demonstrating for voters' rights and freedom for African-Americans.

Lynching was still the law of the land in some rural southern communities. Another group of young men and young women were emerging as a force in the area also. They called themselves 'The Black Panthers', and their beliefs and their attitude was directed to protecting the rights of African Americans and liberating poor and under privileged people from what they deemed and murderous, racist and oppressive government. The organization is considered one of the first groups in U.S. history to militantly struggle for ethnic minority and working class emancipation.

Even though the members did not formally adopt the name 'Black Panthers' until 1966, Huey Newton and Bobby Seale were activists in the Bay area. A faction whose agenda was the revolutionary establishment of *real* economic, social, and political equality across gender and color lines. The Panthers demanded, as stated in their ten point platform: 'freedom and self-determination, full employment for all Black people, restitution for slave labor and mass murder of Black people, decent housing, education to give Black people knowledge of self and expose the true history of American society, exemption from military service for all Black men who should not be forced to defend a racist government, an immediate end to police brutality, release from prison for all Black people because they have not received a fair and impartial trial, all Black people who are brought to trial to be tried by a jury of their peers from the Black community and land, bread, housing, education, clothing, justice and peace. As a major political objective, a United Nations supervised plebiscite for Black Americans to determine their will as to their national destiny'.

I was an activist though the airwaves. I supported the civil rights movement by keeping the residents of the area up to date on the movements and developments on the struggle across the country. I would call Dr. King and members of his staff to get live reports on the activities of the day. I am sure the future members of the Black Panthers were in tune with the station and developing strategies of their own to seek the freedom they desired and strived for.

I would play quotations and passages of speeches of Dr. Martin Luther King, Junior. I would play them preceding station breaks and newscasts. The idea caught on and soon radio black stations all over the country were doing the same.

I would follow his movements and give my early morning listeners an up to the minute account. I would occasionally have Dr. King or one of his staff members on the air with me live to let my listeners be told the skirmishes from the front lines. The civil rights movement was exploding throughout nation, and especially in the South. There were lunch-counter sit-ins, voter registration drives, tenant organizing, recruitment, street protest marches and rallies and prayer vigils.

This was the era of Birmingham's Sheriff 'Bull' Connor's time in power. He was well known for his brutal treatment of Blacks during the struggle of the 1960's. The whole world watched as Connor allowed his police dogs to run free dogs and ordered the Birmingham Fire Department to turn high-powered water hoses on the civil rights marchers. At one point, he rode through the streets on top of an armored tank, calling the marchers Niggers and Nigger lovers.

During one of his assaults, I gave over the air, Connor's private telephone number and asked everyone in the Bay Area who was listening, to call him collect. Apparently hundreds did, and he called me at the radio station and threatened to have me arrested for 'malicious mischief'. I taped the intimidating call and played it on the air, and other disc jockeys that followed also played the recording. Only a year earlier, three civil rights workers, James Chaney, Andrew Goodman and Michael Schwermer had disappeared in Mississippi after being stopped for speeding; they were found buried six weeks later.

And a few weeks earlier, on February 18th 1965, Jimmie Lee Jackson, his mother, **Viola Jackson**, and grandfather, eighty-two year old **Cager Lee Jackson**, took part in a protest demonstration led by Reverend **C. T. Vivian** in favor of African American voter registration. State troopers attacked the marchers and both Jackson's mother and grandfather were hit with billy clubs. When Jackson went to help them he was shot in the stomach by a state trooper. Jackson was arrested and charged with assault and battery before being taken to hospital.

Jimmie Lee Jackson died of his wounds on February 26th, 1965, at the Good Samaritan Hospital in Selma. After Jackson's death, Rev. James Bevel of the Southern Christian Leadership Conference (SCLC) decided to hold a protest demonstration by walking from Selma to Montgomery over the Edmund Pettus Bridge in March.

Also, Congress passed the Civil Rights Act declaring discrimination based on race illegal. The times were heated and the long hot summers were just beginning.

Title VII of the 1964 Civil Rights Act prohibits employment discrimination based on race, color, religion, sex and national origin. Although the law was on the books, change did not come. It was still business as usual. So it was past time to take it to the streets.

CHAPTER 7

The Music!

The music of the day was also reflecting the struggles of the movement. The main independent record promoters of the region were Olin Harrison, an African American independent record distributor, and Denny Zeitler, who worked independently for various record labels. There were also the nationals, such as Columbia, MGM, Capitol, Motown, United Artists and others. Most of the announcers in the Bay area had additional lines of businesses or professions. Most were associated either with the entertainment or the music industry.

North Beach was one of the trendiest areas of the city. In the 1950s, Beatniks, entertainers, poets and artists frequented the neighborhood. Today, North Beach is still the Little Italy of the West Coast, and more Chinese was migrating to the area. The Chinese population grew enormously.

Gentrification has now destroyed what was the predominantly African American community. Nearly 500 Black businesses were moved or ruined, and over 4,000 African American families were displaced.

The Fillmore District was like a West Coast Harlem. Thousand of blacks arrived in the Bay area, mostly in the Fillmore District during the early 1940s to work in war manufacturing, and after the war ended, the neighborhood was never the same. It was difficult for them to find decent work in San Francisco outside of domestic labor, except for the war industry.

There were gathering places like Jimbo's Bop City, the New Orleans Swing Club, and the Club Alabam that later became Club Sullivan and Slim Jenkins in Oakland. There was On Fillmore, Elsie's Breakfast Club, Harold Blackshear's Cafe Society, The Favor and The Havana Club. And some other favorites were The Long Bar, The Blue Mirror, Ebony Plaza Hotel and the Booker T. Washington Hotel.

The rent was cheap and most artists either lived in the area or spent time there. It was the place to be. It was the center of Black culture. Fillmore Street became the "Harlem West" beginning in the 1940's. The Fillmore Theatre was the West Coast Apollo and if you wanted to be seen you had to hang out around Fillmore Street and Geary Blvd. It was the way of life. The big transformation started in 1965, the year that I left San Francisco for St. Louis.

The jocks at KSOL and KDIA were really popular in the Bay Area. Instead of doing record hops, most of the regions personalities actually appeared live in the nightspots up and down the peninsula. Some had club acts and most were the master or mistress of ceremony for the venues that featured live acts.

I gave several shows in San Francisco as well as in Redwood City, Mountain View and East Palo Alto. East Palo Alto comprised the largest African American community on the peninsula. It is now, as it was then, a working class community with some, if not most of the inhabitants, persons who migrated from the South.

THE MIDNIGHTERS
EXCLUSIVELY ON . . . . . . FEDERAL RECORDS

One of the groups that I was fond of and promoted was *The Olympics.* The Olympics was one of the hottest groups in the 50's and the 60s. A couple of their biggest hits were "Western Movies", released in May 1958, that hit both the R&B and the pop charts. The other was "Baby Hully Gully". They also did "Big Boy Pete", "Shimmy Like Kate", "Dance By The Light Of The Moon", "Little Pedro" and "The Slop".

I noticed the deterioration and degeneration of the music industry in 1964. I remember in 1950 when Diana Washington's 'Long John Blues' was banned from the airways because the lyrics were too suggestive. The same thing happened in 1954 when Hank Ballard and the Midnighters released "Work with me Annie", and Dean Martin's 'Wham Bam Thank You Mam" was banned in 1951.

I was noticing the content of records that were on the national charts with tasteless and vulgar subject matter. I really was shocked that there was not a public outcry during this period. In 1954, Ruth Thompson, a Congressional representative introduced legislation meant to ban the mailing of certain "pornographic" records through the U.S. mail.

In September, Billboard magazine targeted R&B songs that they suggested 'contained double entendre references to sex'. Because of this magazine report, police in Long Beach, California, and Memphis, Tennessee, impounded juke-boxes and charged their owners. The next month, Memphis radio station WDIA and several other large popular music radio stations banned several songs for their *sexually suggestive lyrics*. "WDIA said, "in the interest of good citizenship, for the protection of morals and our American way of life does not consider this record, 'Work with me Annie' fit for broadcast on WDIA. We are sure all you listeners will agree with us".

R&B artists and companies were sought out to punish and censor. Variety magazine ran a series on R&B songs they said contained obscene lyrics, and called for censorship of the recording industry, and the CBS television network canceled Alan Freed's Rock 'n Roll Dance Party after a camera showed Frankie Lymon of Frankie Lymon & The Teenagers, dancing with a white girl.

Soon, the music was full of allusions to sex, drugs, and booze and it seemed that no one cared, except for a few groups that wanted censorship. The music was seeping into mostly African American communities and the promoters and lovers of hard rock.

Federal deregulation of the radio industry began during President Ronald Reagan's administration. Reagan began reversing regulation laws; he alleviated the public interest and equal-time provisions of the FCC rules and regulations, and methodically destroyed media restraints and opened the floodgates for the rich to more or less raid the broadcast business. Consequently, only a few companies control the airwaves, therefore they manipulate what millions of people hear, see and read.

The cultural and political ramifications were extensive, by the acquisition of media ownership by a few numbers of corporations and individuals, mostly his friends and contributors. In a single generation, the administration had changed the system and had implemented a brand new form of domination and underhanded deception.

The type and style of music played on the radio has worsened dramatically, as top 40 programmed stations overplayed artists and songs that the record companies had suggested, and tunes that were usually bought and paid for by the record companies. The troubles can be traced to deregulation under the Reagan administration.

Gospel and Religious music, and Negro spirituals played an important part in the changes that took places from the 40's until the present. The music had a dramatic effect on programming especially on southern stations, but it played a fundamental role in the program day of all African American oriented outlets. The father of Gospel Music, pianist and composer Thomas A. Dorsey, helped gospel music come into being. He nurtured and set the standards for gospel performers Mother Willie Mae Ford Smith, Mahalia Jackson, Sister Rosetta Tharpe, Alex Bradford, Cleophus Robinson, James Cleveland, Sallie Martin, Martha Bass, The Caravans, The Swan Silver Tones, Marion Williams, the Gay Sisters, the Soul Stirrers, the original Gospel Harmonettes, The Mighty Clouds of Joy, Clara Ward, Wings Over Jordan Choir, Shirley Caesar, The Dixie Hummingbirds, and The Five Blind Boys of Mississippi and Alabama. These are just a few of the untold number of artists, writers and producers as well as the performers.

Quartets were really big on gospel stations and on the religious segments of the R&B stations. Gospel music was changing rapidly. As blacks traveled to large cities in the North, South and West, more music was exposed to not only the African American community, but to many whites as well. With a growing black economy an up-and-coming metropolitan style, gospel music became one of the most popular genres on the air.

Choirs and coral groups were also recording songs that touched the souls of the masses and nearly every gospel radio program featured at least one. Choirs began to get bigger and bigger, and accompanied by piano or organ, bass, drums, tambourine, guitar and even strings and horns became quite common as well. Gospel radio stations started broadcasting soloists, duets, trios and quartets on nearly every daily show, and some would feature preachers delivering full, unedited sermons. These broadcasts sometimes were the most popular programs on certain radio stations.

The gospel announcer was always chosen to emcee certain religious programs at churches, auditoriums and other venues where concerts were held. The music was growing and Black and white station owners were noticing the revolutionary transformations. They recognized the money making potential of the style and began to capitalize on this development. They recognized it had become an integral part of the African American worship and entertainment experience.

The Black gospel disc jockey showed the power of radio and the significance of spiritual broadcasting to the black community. Nearly every radio station programming to the Black community had a segment devoted to religious broadcasting.

CHAPTER 8

Crossover Music!

The music charts reflected the changes from R&B to pop. The term 'crossover' was not that well known, and the terminology was not that well defined. *Crossover* in the music business simply meant that one genre would or could be played on a radio station or music program that does not usually play that particular type of music. Some thought that "crossover" artists were stealing the music and threatening the integrity of the business. Of course, crossover is important to us in terms of airplay for African American artists because it insures a larger audience for exposure. True crossover music is music, which happens to sell a lot to urban and top 40 markets.

"Crossover," simply means a greatly expanded audience. Crossover music has been a big item in the music industry since the 1950s, but in the 1960s, white Americans heard more and fell in love with soul music, by means of listening to the many African American radio stations emerging across the country. Stax, Motown and Atlantic Records as well as the many independent black companies contributed to the trend. This is when the white 'crossover' or 'blue-eyed soul' artists appeared, such as The Righteous Brothers, Van Morrison and Carole King.

During this period, especially in the 1950's, it was widespread in the industry for a white artist to cover a song that had originally been recorded by a black artist. These recordings usually were not as good as the original but it was the white artist's version that would be promoted by the disc jockeys and the record companies.

Crossover had always happened between black and white musicians. Crossover composers, musicians and artists were always undergoing crossover eagerness.

Some Black artists were played on white stations before the occurrence of crossover crept into the industry. Louis Armstrong, The Ink Spots, Billie Holiday, The Mills Brothers, Ella Fitzgerald, Duke Ellington and Count Basie were played because they amused and entertained whites. The 1950's R&B artists and rock & roll performers and early 1960's music explosion was an entire different story. Blues, boogie-woogie, jazz, swing, and Negro gospel were the targets of the music moguls.

JACKIE WILSON
Brunswick Records

Personal Manager
Nat Tarnopol

UNIVERSAL ATTRACTIONS INC.
200 W. 57 ST, N.Y. 19 N.Y.

JAMES BROWN

FOR BOOKINGS CONTACT
UNIVERSAL ATTRACTIONS INC.
200 WEST 57TH STREET
N. Y. C.   JU 2-7575

Those who slipped through included Chuck Berry, Ray Charles, Sam Cooke, Jackie Wilson, Bo Didley, Little Richard, Fats Domino and Lloyd Price. Actually, white artists imitating and copying Black artists were a starting point of the phenomenon. And those whites that sounded Black also had an impact on the occurrence. The biggest and most prominent was Elvis Presley. And there were other like Buddy Holly, the Righteous Brothers and Roy Orbison.

Dick Clark's *American Bandstand* had a great impact on the industry as well as the television programs like Hullabaloo, Shindig, The Ed Sullivan Show and a small number of others.

"**Shindig!**" began in 1964, featuring rock 'n' roll and soul acts during prime time. The very first show starred Sam Cooke. Other African Americans who appeared included Chuck Berry, Louis Armstrong. Major Lance, James Brown, Ike and Tina Turner and Marvin Gaye.

American Bandstand initially aired on the ABC network on Monday, 5 August 1957. Dick Clark understood that black recording artists performed much of the music on the program, so he was adamant on racially integrating the show.

Ed Sullivan was one of the main influences on the music scene in the late 50s and early 60s. He had not only adults watching his show every Sunday night, but millions of teenagers, and that reality only was a record promoter and artist dream.

Sullivan, through his television show, helped launch the careers of Elvis Presley and The Beatle's. He respected African American culture and openly welcomed and supported black performers throughout his career, including Louis Armstrong, Diana Ross, James Brown, Bill "Bojangles" Robinson, The Temptations, Ethel Waters and Richard Pryor.

The Hullabaloo musical variety television program aired for only two seasons in 1965 and 1966. It was not as popular as Shindig but it gave some limited exposure to a few black artists. Diana Ross, Marvin Gaye and Leslie Uggams made appearances on the show.

There were a few Black artists exposed on pop or white stations. Most of the Motown acts, such as The Supremes, Marvin Gaye, Martha and the Vandellas, The Temptation and The Miracles, but other, less established or independent labels found themselves scuffling for airplay. Many of the top 40 stations were not aware or just did not care of the strides Black people were making. They ignored the personal struggles most African Americans had to endure just to become a part of or remain in the industry. Another indication of the transformation the industry was experiencing.

Bernie Hayes, Jim Gates, Donn Johnson and Eugene Record of the Chi-Lites

Some of the artists and their hits affected were 'Under The Boardwalk—The Drifters', 'My Guy—Mary Wells', 'No Particular Place To Go—Chuck Berry', '20-75—Willie Mitchell', 'Ain't Nothing You Can Do—Bobby Bland', and 'God Bless Our Love—Gene Chandler'.

Songs replacing the R&B selections were 'Be Anything (But Be Mine)—Connie Francis', 'As Usual—Brenda Lee'. 'The House Of The Rising Sun—the Animals', 'Everybody Loves Somebody—Dean Martin', 'Glad All Over—Dave Clark Five', 'Rag Doll—Four Seasons', 'You Really Got Me—the Kinks' and 'Love Me Do—Beatles'.

This is a sampling of what can happen to people who are not in power. When you accept as true the concept of Black Radio, you imagine *personality* radio; public figures from your community, who love and understand the music that you love. Local stars that care about you and try to satisfy your musical and cultural tastes.

These were volatile times in the San Francisco Bay Area. Some of the signs of the times were the constant police harassments of homosexuals. One case in point was the January 1, 1965 New Year's Eve costume ball at California Hall to raise funds for the Council on Religion and the Homosexual. The local police department hassled the participants, nearly causing a riot. Other incidents at the Berkeley Campus of the University of California were almost daily occurrences. The Black Panthers were active and Haight-Ashbury was fast becoming the capital of the avant-garde.

On April 2, 1965, the KSOL Soul Brothers presented a huge Rhythm and Blues concert at the Cow Palace in San Francisco. It was called '**Soul Night at the Palace**', and it was a monumental success. The show featured **Solomon Burke, Jackie Ross, The Supremes, The Temptations, Alvin Cash and the Crawlers, Walter Jackson, The Chi Lites, The Artistics, The Marvelletes and Bobby Freeman. Sly Stone,** who was one of our jocks, lead the band, and we, the jocks acted as masters of ceremonies. In the lobby, and who accompanied us back stage was an up and coming vocal duo that called themselves **Sonny and Cher.**

Solomon Burke is a master of rhythm and blues, rock 'n' roll, gospel and even country music, and is a key figure of the *soul genre.* His credentials are immaculate.

Jackie Ross was celebrating her big monster hit *Selfish One* and she performed several other tunes that eventually became favorites of music lovers all over the world.

Alvin Cash was from St. Louis and primarily and dancer. He had formed a song and dance group with three of his brothers, *the crawlers,* doing tap and soft shoe and other types. Andre Williams produced his hit "Twine Time" and Alvin became a favorite all across the nation. Alvin left us on November 21, 1999.

Jackson 5

The Marvelletes had two big hits on the KSOL record hit list; '**Danger heartbreak ahead**' and '**Please Mr. Postman**'. They moved the crowd almost to the point of frenzy.

Walter Jackson performed on crutches but you would never know it. He was the victim of polio, but he drove a car and virtually ignored his disability. He at one time drove me to Memphis to St. Louis and back. Walter performed like the professional that he was. He sang "It's All Over", "Welcome Home", "That's What Mama Said," and "Funny" among others. He tore the audience up. Walter joined the ancestors in 1983.

Bobby Freeman teamed up with Sly Stone and put on a show with '*Do You Want To Dance*' and '*C'mon And Swim*' and a few other songs that made Bobby so popular.

The Artistics were some of my best friends from my hometown of Chicago. The Artistics, Robert Dobyne, Aaron Floyd, Curt Thomas, Laurence Johnson, and Jesse Bolian, were formed in 1958 at Marshall High School. Major Lance in fact discovered them. They showed the crowd that they were as talented and as smooth as any group recording during that period.

The Chi Lites were formed in Chicago in 1960 and originally called the Hi-Lites, the group featured, Eugene Record, Robert 'Squirrel' Lester, Creadel 'Red' Jones and Marshall Donald Thompson. They almost stole the show with their smooth sound and strategic maneuvers. They got the crowd moving. Eugene Record died in September, 2005.

The story of the Supremes and the Temptations is one of the most repeated legends in show business. **The Supremes** started out as a quartet known as the Primettes, a sister group to accompany the Primes for stage performances. Florence Ballard, Mary Wilson and Diana Ross are legends. They were dressed meticulously and performed the same way.

The Temptations were the result of several groups merging in 1960. Eddie Kendricks and Paul Williams formed the Cavaliers in Birmingham, Alabama. In 1959 Otis Williams formed The Elegants consisting of Elbridge Bryant, Melvin Franklin, his cousin Richard Street, and Albert Harrel and changed their name to the **Primes**. Later, Otis changed the name again to The Temptations and the rest is history. Their string of hit songs and classic Temptation moves had the spectators in the palm of their hands.

After the show at the Cow Palace, I was convinced that soul music was just as high-quality, enjoyable, and maybe superior than ever, and there was no reason that this long-established and timed honored art form should be treated disrespectfully, and segregated, secluded and isolated from the so-called mainstream.

It was the majority, but not all of white record company executives that was responsible for and continue to keep black artist relegated to a second-class status in the music and recording industry. They want complete, exclusive control of this multi-billion dollar business. But most of the artist opposed the separations. Black and white musicians encouraged and influenced each other. The playing field was never level, but the players had mutual admiration. Separation in the early recording industry affected the treatment and inequality of money between blacks and whites. Young White audiences listened to black performers on the radio and occasionally went to their dances or concerts, but it was not something they would reveal to their parents or elders. It was like a secret society for those who loved and enjoyed the music.

Record companies make their business and economic decisions based on sales, regardless of preserving the integrity of ones ethnicity or culture. Even the dynamics of protests by some artists, recording songs of revolution, only aided the record companies by adding to their bank accounts. African Americans on the company rosters were not necessarily viewed as artists and entertainers; rather they were treated as stepchildren. Competition is intense, and the bottom line is profit. They are not interested in enriching ones refinement, making the world more diverse. They are not interested in education or removing stereotypes. They are in business only to make money and they will market their product by any means necessary.

The white record companies and white radio stations were forming an alliance that was excluding the needs of black people and black peoples wants and desires. The warnings were clear but some did not recognize these signals. I was fortunate to be aware of the trends, and I wanted to inform and influence the changes that were coming, but I was not in a position to do so as a disc jockey with no real administrative power. I also had a disagreement with the production manager at KSOL. It was a silly dispute over an automobile and I lost faith and confidence in the organization at the station so I began looking for other places and stations to relocate.

I auditioned at KDAY in Los Angeles. They had been a pop all white station but had switched to an R&B format. Alan Freed was once one of their jocks. KDAY was a daytime AM station at the time. The audition did not work out so I went over to KGFJ. Bill Mercer, known as "Rosko", and The Magnificent "Burn, Baby! Burn" Montague were personalities on the station.

Magnificent Montague I had known and worked with in Chicago. He had worked in New York, and Los Angeles in the 1950s to the mid-1960s. In Los Angeles in 1965 Montague when the Watts riots erupted, he began using the term Burn, *Baby! BURN!* Politicians and community leaders begged him to stop using the slogan to quell the violence.

I was offered the position at KDAY but when I returned to the Bay Area, Ron (Johnny Rabbit) Elz, called me and offered me an announcing position at KATZ in St. Louis. Although he was originally from St. Louis, Ron was a dj at another station in the Bay area. He heard me on the air in San Francisco and called me up to offer me the position at KATZ.

Elz had a long distinguished career in St. Louis before he moved to the West Coast. He was the original Johnny Rabbit at St. Louis station KXOK. When he left California in 1965, he took the job a Johnny American at KATZ. He was also format creator, broadcast school owner, record company representative, program director, newspaper editor and columnist. New York based Laclede Broadcasting out of New York owned KATZ. When I received the call, from Elz I felt it was an offer I could not refuse. I left Palo Alto for St. Louis on April 19th, 1965.

CHAPTER 9

Meet Me In St. Louis!

I took the northern route again. It took two and a half days, this time coming through Sacramento, and spending a few hours to play the slot machines in Reno, and then proceeding through Lake Tahoe, Salt Lake City, and over the Rockies and resting for the night in Denver. The next morning it was back on Interstate 70 East through Kansas, which seemed like it had no eastern border, and finally Kansas City, Missouri. After experiencing some Gates Barbeque again, it was back on the highway finally reaching St. Louis around 9 p.m. on April 21st.

St. Louis Black Radio has a rich and illustrious history. St. Louis played a profound, powerful and passionate journey on the path of historical significance. Establishing the city as a leader in supplying the Black population with entertainment, knowledge, social news, and civic events; and later, calmed the violence attributed to the assignation of Dr. Martin Luther King, Jr.; Black radio also supported African American religious and spiritual organizations.

The major St. Louis stations that offered programs and personality shows aimed at the 'Negro Market' in the early days were (a) **KATZ-AM 1600** that began broadcasting on January 3, 1955. The station was located on the second floor of the Arcade Building at 8th and Olive Streets, in downtown St. Louis. (b) **KXLW**—AM, went on the air on January 1, 1947, but did not start broadcasting exclusively to the African American community until Richard R. Miller started that phase of his operation in the early 60's. He also owned **KADI**-FM. The stations were located on Bomparte Avenue in the Brentwood area off Manchester Road; (c) **KWK**: Ed Wilson and Gil Newsome's 'Bandstand Review' and Tom Dailey's 'Recall It and Win.' programs had made the station a powerhouse before the station became an R&B outlet. It was called 'one of the finest radio stations in the United States'. The station lost its license because of an alleged phony contest and went silent for several years.

KWK-AM 1380. KWK re-opened in the TV 30 Building at Tucker and Cole streets in 1969, but later re-located to Hall Street (500 Terminal Row) in North St. Louis near the Mississippi River. Across the River there was **WTMV 1490 A M** that later became **WBBR, WAMV and** at the present time is **WESL**.

No portrayal or depiction of St. Louis radio would be complete without the recognition of the significance and importance of gospel and religious music, and the personalities who pioneered the domain.

Top Photo-Bernie Hayes
Bottom photo-Barbara Burton, Count Basis and Robert BQ

Nearly all of the local stations that provided programming to the African American community incorporated a significant amount of religious line-ups in each day's schedule. *Dr. Thomas A. Dorsey*, the most influential figure ever to impact the gospel music scene, had a major influence on the St. Louis gospel occurrence. The author of "Take My Hand, Precious Lord" and "Peace in the Valley", and the founder of the National Convention of Gospel Choirs and Choruses, now known as the Gospel Music Workshop, was also a pioneering force in the St. Louis gospel community. He helped launch the careers of legends including *Mahalia Jackson, Sallie Martin*, and the foremost influence in St. Louis gospel music, **Mother Willie Mae Ford Smith**. They helped create the genre in which religious and gospel music evolved. The 1982 film 'Say Amen Somebody', was filmed in St. Louis and featured Dr. Dorsey, Mother Smith, Sallie Martin, Zella Jackson Price, The O'Neal Twins, DeLois Barrett Campbell, Michael and Bertha Smith, Geneva Gentry and others too numerous to name.

Local artists who gained national attention from the St. Louis area are Martha Bass, (mother of Fontella Bass), Brother Joe Mays, Dello Thedford, Reverend Cleophus Robinson, The O'Neal Twins and Zella Jackson Price.

There are *too many* gospel and religious announcers to name, because **all of** the personalities at one time or another played gospel music, but the *most notable* were Wynetta Lindsay, Leonard Morris, Rev. Cleophus Robinson, George 'The G" Logan, Zella Jackson Price, Ruby Somerville, Devan Strong, Minister Hosea Gales, Brother Columbus Gregory, who is currently on the air at KIRL—AM in St. Charles, and Merdean Fielding-Gales, who is presently featured on the nationally syndicated **Bobby Jones Television Show.** As the Black gospel announcer was up-and-coming, Sister Rosetta Tharpe took the music to another level. She starred in nightclubs singing gospel songs. The number of quartets began to grow, and local announcers began featuring them live in the studios of their respective stations. Rhythm and Blues music would not have evolved without the gospel and religious connection.

I picked up KATZ around 60 miles from the city. I heard Jerome Dixon doing a live remote broadcast from The Top Cat Lounge in the city's west end. I drove to the radio stations studio, which was located in the Arcade Building at, 8th and Olive Streets in downtown, St. Louis. I was looking for the program director, Robert B.Q. Burris, but he was not around. I met the engineer on duty, Harry Crawford and he put out a call for B.Q. but to no avail. So I got directions from the engineer and went to the remote broadcast where Dixon was working.

His program was called "Night Beat Down Rhythm Street", and as I entered, he invited me to sit in with him and he introduced me as the new jock in town. This was the night I met Milton "Buddy" Lonesome, a popular journalist and well-respected businessman in the region. He was the Editor of the St. Louis Argus Newspaper. The St. Louis Argus newspaper is the oldest Black Business in Missouri, founded in 1912 by Joseph Mitchell and his brother William Mitchell. After 1945, William Mitchell's widow, Nannie Mitchell-Turner became the president of the Argus Publishing Company. Buddy Lonesome had an important function at the Argus.

I stayed the night in the Carousel Motel on Kingshighway and Natural Bridge. In 1965 it was a first class, first-rate facility, with the latest modern services and conveniences. The following morning I checked in at the radio station and actually went on the air that same day. My shift was from two to six in the afternoon, Monday through Saturday.

The next morning, I got a glimpse at the unfinished Gateway Arch. It was an enormous structure, gleaming in the sun like new-minted silver. Construction of the Arch began in 1963. It is now 630 feet high, but at this time it was no more than 400 feet high. The Gateway Arch is part of the Jefferson National Expansion Memorial. It also houses the Museum of Westward Expansion, and St. Louis' Old Courthouse. I saw the slave blocks attached to the Courthouse where my ancestors were sold as slaves, and I remember then as now, a cold chill engulfs my spirit and anger twinges in my heart. The Old Courthouse, built in 1839, is also where the first two trials of the Dred Scott case were held in 1847 and 1850.

Civil rights activist Percy Green, and his civil rights organization known as ACTION, was also protesting department stores that did not serve blacks at lunch counters. He and Richard Daly had climbed the Gateway Arch the year before protesting job discrimination during the construction of the monument. The Arch was completed on October 28, 1965.

I was introduced to the office staff and the few announcers who happened to be at the radio station. The general manager, Marty Brown was in the hospital. George Lasker had taken over his managerial duties while he was recuperating. Robert B.Q., the program director, acquainted me with Beatrice Payne, Patricia McCottrel, Barbara Burton and other office personnel. The only other announcer at the station was Doug Eason, who held down the 10 a.m. to 2 p.m.

The daily line up began at 5:00 a.m. with The Leonard Morris' Gospel show. Leonard started with KATZ in 1963. At 6:00 a.m., Robert BQ followed Leonard Morris with the Early Bird Show. In 1964, he succeeded Dave Dixon as program director of KATZ. *BQ* was responsible for hiring and supervising some of the stations most noted personalities, and he is credited with establishing the station as a national powerhouse. BQ was also responsible for recording some of the areas most noted groups. He was an innovator in multi-track phonograph recordings. He started his career in the late 50's as an engineer at WTMV in East St. Louis, Illinois. The call letters were later known as WBBR, and is now WESL.

Doug (The Leprechaun) Eason, who embarked on his broadcasting career in 1964as a newscaster at KXLW. Doug moved to KATZ in early 1965 as a newscaster. Later that year he became the mid-morning DJ. "_The Leprechaun_" eventually became general manager of KATZ. He hosted 'The Black Circle Hour' television dance show on Channel 30. Eason also managed WESL in East St. Louis, Illinois and eventually bought a radio station in Mobile, Alabama. He moved to California after his stay in Mobile, and then to Kansas City, Missouri where he managed a local station.

I followed Doug Eason. Ron (Johnny American) Elz, Ron Elz was the first "Johnny Rabbitt" on KXOK. He was a dj in California and is responsible for me coming to St. Louis. He worked at St. Louis stations KSHE, WIL, WRTH and several others. He is the consummate professional.

Buster Jones was the early evening dj on KATZ. He was a favorite with the teens and did record hops constantly. He was also a recording artist. He moved to Philadelphia and eventually would up in Los Angeles. He hosted Soul Unlimited television specials for Dick Clark Productions and was featured in more than 50 movies.

Jerome Dixon with Night Beat Down Rhythm Street. Jerome worked at the Post Office and broadcasted at night or early evenings. He replaced his brother Dave Dixon who hosted the program before his tragic death in 1964. Jerome was killed in an auto accident near Chicago in 1968.

Top photo-Donnie Brooks
Bottom photo: E. Rodney Jones-Doug Eason—Albert King

Spider Burks was on the air in St. Louis from 1947 through the early 70s. He worked at KXLW, KATZ, KADI and KSTL. He was the first after Wiley Price who began in 1945. Spider was a pioneer in the business, and opened doors for those who followed. His preference was jazz, and he established himself as one of the nations most well informed of this genre. Spider began in 1947 at KXLW and later moved to KSTL and KATZ. While at KXLW, he was one of the highest paid African American disc jockeys in the country. His sponsors included some of the regions largest companies, including Anhueser—Busch. He was noted for his flashy dress and expensive cars, but he was an *adept businessman*. He also owned or held interests in several nightclubs and other hot spots around town. He was a favorite in the nightclubs, and jazz and music lovers around St. Louis and the county attended his live broadcasts.

Barbara Burton-Robert BQ

Roscoe McCrary-Chuck Berry

Spider was strictly a jazz dj, and he did live shows from around the area with some of the nations leading jazz performers. I replaced him in June of 1965 as the jazz personality announcer at Leo's Blue Note Club in East St. Louis, Illinois. Spider died in 1974.

In 1952, **Wiley Price** began his broadcasting career in St. Louis, playing big band sounds and the jazz music of the day. Price refused to play most secular rhythm and blues music, and preferred the *modern and jazz classics*. Artists such as Lena Horne, Louis Armstrong, Count Basie, Dizzy Gillespie, Duke Ellington, Miles Davis, Sarah Vaughn, Billie Holliday and Billy Eckstein were some of his favorites. He established an audience in and for the African American community that the mainstream medium *ignored*.

Later, personalities such as 'Little Old Roscoe' McCrary and, Amos 'Panyo' Dotson, George 'The Rocking Mr. G.' Logan and a host of others emerged on *Illinois and Missouri* **radio stations WBBR, WTMV, KATZ and KXLW.**

Lou 'Fatha' Thimes started as a DJ at **KATZ** in 1958. He went to KXLW in 1960 where he was a favorite among all sets and classes. He had previously been a comedian with the comedy team of 'Lou and Blue." Thimes is known for his love *and* knowledge of the blues, and has been a favorite of the masses all of these years. He is a real pioneer in the St. Louis radio market, of both the blues *and* urban music. He has worked also at **KADI, KKSS, Majic 108, and WESL** and is currently at **KDHX-88.1**

Gabriel relieved me at three o'clock in the morning following my shift at the Blue Note Club. He started his broadcasting career in 1951. He is a musician, entrepreneur, producer and promoter. He is an authority on the blues and Negro gospel music, and gave several singers and musicians their introduction to the radio and music industries.

The weekend featured Wynetta Lindsey, one of the first and most popular of gospel announcers. She started at KATZ in 1963 and remained until 1969. Devan Strong who was also a remote broadcast engineer, who along with

German Massenberg, produced and directed several churches remote broadcasts, including the church headed by The Reverend Cleophus Robinson. He had his own a coast-to-coast gospel television show for more than 25 years as well as his radio broadcasts. He was known as 'the worlds greatest gospel singer', and recorded for several record labels, producing many hits. His church had one of the largest congregations in the city.

KATZ's major rivalry was with KXLW. Richard R. Miller bought it in 1959. The station had only 1,000 watts of power and located at 1320 AM, compared to KATZ with 5000 watts on 1600 AAM. Spider Burks was the first African American on KXLW. He worked their form 1947 to 1956.

The other jocks on KXLW were Lou 'Fatha' Thimes, who started as a DJ at KATZ in 1958. He went to KXLW in 1960 where he was a favorite among all sets and classes. He had previously been a comedian with the comedy team of 'Lou and Blue."

Gracie was also a personality on KXLW. Willa Mae Gracy Lowry was St. Louis' first St. Louis African-American woman personality on KATZ-AM. Gracy started in the late 50's, performing office and secretarial duties and finally became one of the best known and loved radio personalities in St. Louis. She is credited with *instituting regular remote* broadcasts of her program at KATZ. She left KATZ in the early 60's to work as a DJ at KXLW and KADI, and later *returned* to the KATZ airways. Gracy became the first national secretary for the African-American fraternal association NARA (National Association of Radio Announcers, which later became NATRA). She also owned Pierre's Record Shop and had a gasoline station franchise. Gracy passed on December 18, 2003.

Friends of KATZ 1600 Very Own:
Salutes

GRACY!

Sunday, NOVEMBER 8, 1992   2 P.M. · 6 P.M.

Spruills International Catering Inc.
1101 No. Jefferson Ave., St. Louis, MO

Other personalities included George "The G" Logan. He was one of the most talented personalities in St. Louis during the late 50s and early 60s. He was as skillful playing Gospel as he was at R&B. He was a true master of the radio arts.

Jimmy Bishop, who later became Program Director for WDAS Radio in Philadelphia, had previously been a dj at the station but he left in 1964, a few months before I arrived in the city.

Later Steve Byrd joined the station. He was imported from Philadelphia, where he was a student and nearly a carbon copy of Jimmy Bishop.

Other popular Deejays worked at KATZ. One of the favorite young announcers in the area was **Al Waples,** A St. Louis native who began his radio career at KATZ in 1966 as a newscaster. Al was a recording artist as well. In 1970, he left KATZ to become a DJ at KWK before leaving for Philadelphia, and eventually landing in Los Angeles. Waples was the national network announcer for the Jackson 5 Television Program, and became one of the best-known DJ's in Los Angeles. He left L.A. to move to the Mid-South where he is currently working as an announcer and personality.

Al Waples

James Earl 'Gentleman Jim' Gates: The 'Brown Eyed Scorpio' as he is often called, started his radio career in 1968 at KATZ-AM. "Gentleman Jim" went to KWK in 1971 where he was established as one of the most popular personalities in the area. He and I hosted the **Black Circle Hour** television dance program and later **The Soul Brotherhood** television dance show as noted in the book. A few years later, Gates became a co-owner of Radio Station WESL in East St. Louis, Illinois. After a brief stint in Detroit, Gates returned to St. Louis. He was interim manager for KATZ in the mid 80's, and later worked at Majic 108 FM.

Top Photo: Jim Gates
Bottom photo: Soul Brotherhood-Channel 30

Top Photo: Soul Brotherhood
Bottom photo: Spider Burks and Leo Gooden

KATZ did a lot of local small budget promotions. One of the favorites of the listeners and the deejays was 'Sweet 16 Day'. On the 16th of each month, the station would play old records from years past. It was a real hit with the public. Another marketing tool was called 'The KATZ MAN is on the Prowl", and if the fan recognized the **KATZ MAN**, the enthusiast would win prizes, oftentimes cash.

Neither KATZ nor KXLW had the big bucks like the general market stations, but they had loyal admirers. The listeners were true to the stations and would support them whenever possible. While the other stations were giving away large sums of money, the two Black stations gave the minimal but kept their devoted fans.

A few weeks after I started at KATZ, Leo Gooden, who owned the **Blue Note Club**, approached me. I had known Leo from his association with Ernie Leaner in Chicago. The nightclub was located at 4300 Missouri Avenue in East St. Louis Illinois, and featured live broadcasts nightly over KATZ. He wanted me to become the announcer from his place, replacing Spider Burks who was leaving.

The Blue Note was the most popular place in the area for live entertainment and they were open until 5:00 a.m. I appreciated the opportunity to do a jazz show, plus the increase in salary played a significant part in my decision. The live broadcast was from Midnight to three in the morning.

The club featured 'Leo's Five', a combo that featured several well-known musicians that included Don James, Larry Prothro, Eddie Fisher, Freddie Jackson and Hammet Bluett, JR. and Kenny Rice. Oliver Nelson, Yusef Lateef, Redd Foxx, Lou Rawls and other nationally recognized entertainers and politicians were regulars there.

The radio audience incorporated up and coming black and white musicians and entertainers as well as late night revelers and all night workers. It was the after-hours place to be, for dancing and good food and music.

I played R&B in the afternoon and jazz at night. People thought there were two people named Bernie Hayes on KATZ.

At this time, an up and coming singer from Alton, Illinois named Luther Ingram told me that his hometown did not have a record store. He informed me that people from his hometown had to travel nearly 30 miles to St. Louis to buy records. He convinced me to open a record store in Alton, so in late1965, my wife and I opened 'Music World Record Store' at 503 Belle Street in downtown Alton.

By becoming a retail record storeowner, I gained more knowledge of the record, and retail industry, especially as it related to radio and the music industry. I was in competition with one-stops, rack jobbers, other retail outlets and even some bootleggers. I did not get the support from the major distributors because I was African American, nor at my store did they provide marketing and promotion support for their artists. But I understood the reasons and did not let the bigotry in the industry disturb me. I was still a radio personality at the largest R&B station in the region.

The pop alternative to KATZ was KXOK, part of the Todd Storz chain of AM stations. The announcers were Ron Elz and Don Pietromonaco who both at one time were known as 'Johnny Rabbitt'; others were Dick Ulett, Ray Otis, Mort Crowley, Nick Charles, Robert R. Lynn, William D. Rogers, Steven B. Stevens and Bobby Shannon.

The station, labeled 'Radio Park', was located in the African American neighborhood, at 1600 North Kingshighway near Martin Luther King.

During this time KXOK did not play many Black records. They were strictly a pop oriented, top 40 radio station, directing their programming to a general white audience, not realizing that American society was being transformed. It did not care or consider African American intellect or culture. As far as their programming was concerned, African American art, music or history was not worthy or sought after for their station.

In 1965 the other top 40 station was WIL-AM. Some of the personalities associated with WIL were Bob Osborne, Jack Carney, Gary Owens, Bob Hardy, Ron Lundy, Dan Ingram, Dick Clayton, Danny Dark, Gary Stevens, and Nelson Kirkwood.

The station was, in my opinion, more liberal than KXOK, because it, at times, seemed to challenge the stereotypes associated with Blacks and other minorities. They did not give the impression of dividing the relations between Blacks and whites, and their music policy regarding African American artists was more lenient.

The music distributors also reflected this negative attitude toward the Black community and radio personalities and the facilities we worked for. There were several local distributors who sought airplay on the two black oriented stations. Commercial Record Distributors handled the majority of the Motown line and several other major labels. Al Chotin owned it, and they assisted only certain disc jockeys, for it was their policy to service either the music director or the program director, which were usually the same person. Skip Gorman was also a major player who at one time controlled the Motown labels. His operation was also on Washington Avenue, near the corner of 21st Street. He later branched off and became a distributor of independent labels.

Most of the other major labels were across the street from Commercial, headed by Norman Wienstohr and Norman Hofstetter. They were the distributors for Atlantic, Stax and most of the additional brands. There was also Liberty Record Distributors who carried their subsidiary HI records and others. Also, there were a number of 'One Stops'. These are warehouse outlets that sold records at wholesale prices to record stores and department stores and other retail outlets. Pat Blunda and Ted and Zelda Hudson controlled this market in 1965, through Pat's One Stop and Hudson's Embassy Retail and Wholesale Records. They carried all of the major and most independent labels. We were at their mercy for receiving promotional and advance recordings from the record companies, whether they were Black or white. And the white disc jockeys, white radio stations and white record storeowners were always given particular and special treatment.

Whereas the Black record storeowners were charged one price for wholesale records, the white owned stores were offered 'deals', meaning they were offered records at discounted prices.

The number one retailer in St. Louis was Sid Carson, who owned four 'Joe's Music Store's'. All of his retail outlets were in the heart of the black community. He would receive information from the distributors and manufacturers before the other retail dealers and take advantage of these tips. The distributors would alert the white owners and not tell the smaller, black stores of the offers. Therefore the white stores had an advantage by making a higher profit, and attaining a higher standard of living. It was another form of racism in the industry. Lillian Van Hook operated a popular retail store at Easton and Taylor. She experienced the bias and unfairness dispersed by the white wholesalers. She passed in October, 2005. These businessmen did not usually address Law and ethics. They were interested only in how much profit they could make.

Black retailer were constantly trying to keep up with their white counterparts and the playing field was never level. Black stores never attained the market share they deserved.

During this period, Stax Records was one of the largest African-American record companies. They played a pivotal role in bringing about a respect for independent labels. They changed the meaning of self-reliant with the many well-established artists. At one time they were releasing hit after hit on such artist as Rufus Thomas, Luther Ingram, The Barkays, Carla Thomas, Isaac

Hayes, The Emotions, The Mad Lads, Booker T and the MGs, Albert King, Johnnie Taylor and so many more.

Al Isbell, known in the business as Al Bell, bought the company from Jim Stewart and Stewart's sister, Marge Axton. Bell, needing a more lucrative outlet for distributing Stax products, in 1972, Bell contracted and contracted with Columbia Records for distribution. Columbia provided Stax with six million dollars in advance. Al Bell made the arrangement with Clive Davis, then President of Columbia Records. Columbia later changed the agreement with Stax and fired Davis, critically reducing Stax cash flow and putting the company in bankruptcy.

I was a Stax artist at this time. I had recorded "Tribute to A Black Woman", "Cool Strut" and "The Monkey Scratch".

My first apartment in St. Louis was located at 3316 Belt Avenue, and later I purchased a home at 5661 Chamberlain Avenue, in the city's West End neighborhood. I did not know at the time, but I had moved next door to Bill Fields, whom I had worked with at WGES in Chicago. Fields was hosting a talk show at KPLR—TV channel 11.

I was anxious to familiarize myself in this new market and brand new surroundings. I had passed through St. Louis in 1956 on my way to KDBS in Alexandria, Louisiana, and again with Little Walter when returning to Chicago. I remember a restaurant near Union Station that I had dinner once. It was named Crown Café, and I later learned the area was called Mill Creek.

The Mill Creek area became the victim of gentrification in 1950's under the guise of Urban Renewal. This Black neighborhood lost nearly 30,000 residents, consisting of nearly 6000 families, and nearly 1000 churches, businesses, and other establishments, wiping out more black traditions and disrupting the entire social class. The boundaries of Mill Creek Valley ran from 20th Street to Grand, and from Olive Street south to the railroad tracks.

I knew that for Black people in America, radio was the center of communication, and many social and monetary group issues were discussed, that influenced numerous characteristics of their lives on a daily basis. Issues that applied to state and local governments that impacted the African American community were often only printed in Black newspapers or discussed on Black radio stations. Black announcers were considered the griots of the African American community. We were our people's genealogical storytellers. We told and preserved personal stories and perspectives for future generations and carried on a tradition that was centuries old. We provided connections to our past that might otherwise have been lost or discounted.

The music industry was increasingly going through modifications. Black music is an invaluable source of preserving African American history and culture, and we were slowly but surely losing charge. Caucasian artists and Caucasian owned record manufacturers were recording and covering black music, thereby closing the door on the Black writers, producers and performers. I knew that music, art, faith and history, influence cultural values and attitudes, and I saw Blacks about to lose connection with our past, and face an uncertain, dependent future. I recognized the influence of media, and with the changing demographic and socioeconomic diversity and multicultural backgrounds in the Black community, the challenges seemed insurmountable.

I became accustomed and familiar with parts of the city in a short period of time. My popularity soon grew also. Being the new guy in town, I was featured in the Annie Malone May Day Parade. The Annie Malone Children and Family Service Center sponsor it, and figures show each year the affair draws over 200 floats and nearly 60,000 viewers. It is the second largest African American parade in the country, just behind the Bud Biliken Parade in Chicago.

A few months after my arrival, a group of students from Beaumont High School created the first Bernie Hayes Fan Club. I played records at the 1965 Beaumont High School Prom, and shortly afterwards began spinning on a regular basis at Vashon, O'Fallon, Soldan and Sumner High as well. I also was occasionally entertaining in nightclubs and bars around the area.

1965 was an unforgettable year. One of the most unforgettable recollections that I have before moving from California to Missouri was the feuding between factions of the Nation of Islam. On February 21, 1965, Malcolm X was shot to death at a rally of his followers as he delivered a speech in The Audubon Ballroom in Manhattan. His original name was Malcolm Little, and his Muslim name was El-Hajj Malik El-Shabazz.

Although he spent several years in confinement, he moved to Boston in 1946 to live with his sister. He converted to Islam while in prison. In 1952 he went to Chicago to meet the Honorable Elijah Muhammad. He founded Muhammad Speaks Newspaper and became the spokesman for the Nation.

As Malcolm X, he was sent on speaking tours around the country and soon became the most forceful and influential speaker and organizer for the Nation of Islam. It was Malcolm who recruited The Honorable Louis Farrakhan into the organization.

He spoke against the white mistreatment of black people, and advocated the use of violence when necessary for self-protection. In February 1964, The Honorable Elijah Muhammad suspended him when Malcolm described the assassination of President John F. Kennedy as a "case of chickens coming home to roost".

He left the Nation of Islam in March 1964 and formed his own religious group. The next month, he took a pilgrimage to Mecca, and adapted more moderate views of black separatism. In October 1964 he converted to orthodox Islam. The Mounting resentment between Malcolm's followers and the Nation of Islam continued to grow until his death and for years to come.

I met Minister Abraham and later Minister Aziz here in St. Louis a few months later. Minister Aziz now the chief spokesperson for Minister Farrakhan and is now known as Minister Akbar Muhammad.

A few days after Malcolm's assassination, Jimmy Lee Jackson was shot when he went to help his mother and grandfather who were participating in a peaceful march to the Perry County courthouse. The incident prompted the Selma to Montgomery March, where participants were attacked on the Pettus Bridge in Selma, Alabama. The assault focused the Nation's attention on the Selma March, and led to the Voting Rights Act in 1965. Jackson died on February 18th, 1965, three days before Malcolm's death.

Also in 1965, the EEOC, or the Equal Employment Opportunity Commission, began operations officially July 2, 1965 one year after the passage of the 1964 Civil Rights Act.

And George "Father Divine" Baker died. His followers, both Black and white, thought he was God. A 1965 Civil Rights Act was passed and signed by President Lyndon Johnson; Additionally in 1965, as I mentioned earlier, three voting-rights activists, Michael Schwermer, Andrew Goodman and James Chaney, were murdered in Philadelphia, Mississippi. On March 7, 1965, Alabama State Troopers attacked and set dogs upon peaceful marchers crossing the Edmund Pettus Bridge in Selma. They were en route to the state capitol in Montgomery to lobby for voting rights legislation. It was the beginning of Freedom Summer.

On August 11, 1965, a routine traffic stop in South Central Los Angeles provoked residents of the area to initiate the Watts Riots that lasted for six days, and left 34 people dead. Los Angeles did not realize the volatile situation poor people were in, and frantically seeking justice, decided all hope was lost, and decided to burn the city down.

In 1965, Bobby Seale and Huey Newton met while they were attending college. They later formed The Black Panther Party. New York City had a blackout. Nat King Cole also died in 1965. Alan Freed, the disc jockey credited with naming rock & roll died at 42. ABC-TV gave Freed his own nationally televised show, but an incident, which Frankie Lymon danced with a white girl, infuriated ABC's Southern affiliates and they cancelled the show; Edward R Murrow who narrated and produced the radio series Hear It Now and the television show See It Now, Person to Person and Small World, died.

Popular actress Dorothy Dandridge died at 41 in Hollywood of an overdose of sleeping pills. She was the first African American to be nominated as Best

Actress in a motion picture in 1954. She was also married to the dancer Harold Nicholas, of the Nicholas Bros. She starred in "Carmen Jones", "Porgy and Bess", "Bright Road" and "Island In The Sun".

Johnny Lee, the actor who played attorney Algonquin J. Calhoun on the Amos 'n' Andy Television show, died of a heart attack. He was 67. Amos 'N' Andy made the transition from radio to TV in 1951. He was an accomplished actor but never achieved the recognition he deserved.

The Missouri legislature passed the Missouri Public Accommodations Act of 1965, ending discrimination in public facilities and David E. McPherson became the first African American trooper on the Missouri State Highway Patrol.

The **KATZ** studios were located on the 3rd floor of the Arcade Building on 8th and Olive Streets in downtown St. Louis. The facility was a favorite stopping spot for artists on the "chitlin circuit" and nationally known artists as well. Ike and Tina Turner were frequent visitors. Both had lived in St. Louis. And artists on national tours were also regular guests. For example the Spaniels, The Dells, Albert King, The Drifters and The Platters were regular guests at the station.

Regal Sports

Regal Sports Incorporated was the major promoter of soul acts from the early 40s until the mid 80s. They presented every major and upcoming attraction that was available on the 'chitlin' circuit as well as established performers, like Sammy Davis Jr., James Brown, Joe Tex, The Temptations, The Motown Revues, The Stax and Atlantic Record Reviews. They also brought Tom Jones and The Beetles.

Regal Sports was originally known as the 'Don Cuban Social Club'. Brothers Everett and Tom Agnew, Jr., Allie Howard, Claude Kelly, Jesse Johnson, and Joe B. Finney founded the organization. They established the agency in 1937 in a district of the city called 'Peters Ville', that bordered from Jefferson Avenue to Grand Avenue and from St. Louis Avenue to Cass Avenue. The name Regal was assumed after one of the members attended a stage show at Chicago's Regal Theater. They also had a baseball team and a football teams and so they agreed to the name **Regal Sports**. They presented the biggest and best African American entertainers at all of the major venues available to them at that time.

The first act they booked was Count Basie at the Castle Ballroom in March 31, 1941. The ticket prices were $.85 in advance and $1.00 at the door. Also in 1941, the group brought Jimmie Lunsford, Erskine Hawkins, Billie Eckstein, Earl 'Fatha' Hines and Madeline Green to the Keil Auditorium. Other acts the Regal Sports promoted in the early days were Dinah Washington, Brook Benton, Sarah Vaughn, Duke Ellington, Cab Callaway, George Hudson, Andy Kirk and all of the other big name celebrities of the day.

The Regal Sports inspired and motivated other social clubs and individuals to become show promoters. They had a significant impact on the area and paved they way for some white promoters, some of whom later treated the Regal Sports unfairly by over bidding on acts the sports wanted in an attempt to put them out of business. If it was a hit in St. Louis, Regal Sports had them. I became their MC in the late 60s until they disbanded in the late 80s.

The metropolitan area was loaded with nightclubs and dance halls. The Club Rivera at Delmar and Taylor was one of the main entertainment centers when I arrived in 1965. The Cosmopolitan Club in East St. Louis housed Chuck Berry and Johnnie Johnson. There was also the city owned Kiel Auditorium and Kiel Opera House where most of the concerts were held. The St. Louis Hawks played their professional basketball games at Kiel during their tenure in St. Louis from 1955 through 1967.

One of the most popular hotspots in 1965 was **Gaslight Square.** It was a major St. Louis tourist attraction in the early to mid-1960s. It was located in the Central West End, encircling Olive and Boyle Streets. It had tourist appeal with several nightclubs, comedy clubs, bars, art galleries, theatres, antique stores, coffee houses, bookstores, music and social establishments to satisfy all tastes. The Crystal Palace, and the Roaring Twenties Saloon was a couple of the main attractions along Olive Street.

Subsequent to being on the air on KATZ twice a day, in June 1965, I was contacted by Luther Ingram, a young singer and songwriter from Alton, Illinois who told me that his hometown had no retail record store. After investigating several possible locations, I opened 'Music World Records' at 503 Belle Street in the downtown section of Alton.

Alton, Illinois, is one of the oldest settlements in the Midwest. It is located on the north side of the Mississippi River twenty-five miles north of St. Louis. Its history dates back to the middle 1600s. Elijah Parish Lovejoy is best known and remembered for his stand against slavery. After a mob destroyed his press in 1836, he moved to Alton.

Miles Davis was born in Alton, although he grew up grew up in East St. Louis. He played around the St. Louis area with Eddie Randall's Blue Devils when he was young. Former St. Louis Public Schools superintendent Cleveland Hammonds, Jr. is also a native of Alton.

Alton is also known as the home of "the Gentle Giant." **Robert Wadlow,** who was born in 1918, and grew to a height of 8 feet, 11.1 inches.

It was through Music World Records that I again saw the change in the music industry and in Black radio. During the early through mid 60s, the wholesale price for a 45 rpm single was around $.35-$.45 and sold at retail for around $.67-$.87. A 33 rpm LP would cost approximately $1.50 and retail for around $2.98-$3.49, depending on the artist and label.

If a white retailer could buy 100 singles and get 20 free on a 'deal', his cost for the product drops considerably from $35.00 to $28.00, and the business is able to undersell their competition and yet make a profit higher than their competitor. If you multiply these figures by ten, you can see the disproportion and discrimination, and the reason why the black owners prices were higher and their profits lower.

Often the pop or white radio stations were serviced before the black oriented stations with crossover records, thereby allowing the general market facility to claim "heard first on XXXX". This gives the impression that the first to air a particular record or artist is the most significant and best in the market. It was a false impression but one that could determine the stations ratings and either increase or decrease sales, and a station exists only on sales. Sales are the main and sometimes only source of revenue. It is the reason a station is in business.

The salesperson would usually sell the *personalities;* they would sell either the disc jockey or the time slot a particular media magnet was on the air. Often, the talent would get paid extra if a sponsor bought their particular program.

The payment or commission would vary from five percent to twenty-five percent. A lot of variables applied.

Radio technology in the early years is nothing like radio today. AM radio was the most important method of mobile entertainment and every song on the radio was in monaural. The jocks were not only appreciated and respected, but also in some instances, revered. Black oriented radio stations provided African Americans news and information vital to the local community. The newscasters were as important and as popular as the disc jockeys. Black radio news supported the Civil Rights and Black Power movements.

Personalities would actually be a part of the music and keep their audiences entertained and informed. A good *morning* personality would play the best music; keep you up to date on the time and weather and traffic information. Perhaps they would give news of happenings at local schools and announce lunch menus, and talk to their audience and local and national persons of interest. The music would be up-tempo and lively and they would always sound cheerful. The jocks would often sing along with the music or have witty or animated comments while the music played. This style was the forerunner of the rap genre.

CHAPTER 10

Top 40 Vs. Soul Radio

An occurrence in California in 1964 added substantially to the demise of personality and eventually to the destruction of Black Radio, as we knew it. It was called **Boss Radio**. A combination of Boss radio and Top 40 radio were the leading contributors to ending what was a creative, and unifying society. Black radio was a medium that played an influential role in both African American lives and in a broad-spectrum of the dominant culture.

The focus of both Boss Radio and top 40 formats were more music and less talk, and that meant less personality. The stations would arrange a minimum of 14 songs to be played per hour; the announcer was regulated to 15 seconds between songs; the jocks were to introduce one song as the prior song faded out and station jingles were limited to 90 seconds. Advertising spots were limited to 13 minutes per hour news reports occurred 20 minutes past the hour rather than at the hour and most songs were played back to back to deny listeners from switching the dial.

In the mid-sixties, the formats at KATZ and KXLW remained as they had been prior to the Boss and top 40-system that dominated pop and general market radio. Because the black oriented stations were receiving a share of local and national advertising dollars, the station owners were fairly content with their revenue dollars. Black stations never expected to earn what the white stations made. The advertising agencies and local retail businesses never gave parity to stations serving the Black market. Advertising is an industry that is paid to discriminate, and racial bias is a multifaceted problem. Radio stations that focused on minorities' consistently received fewer ad dollars per listener, causing black owned stations to get a disproportionately small amount of advertising revenue.

We as black deejays were paid less than our white counterparts also. Blacks, because of discrimination in the industry, earned from 30-60 percent of what white deejays earned. That figure in some instances, hold true today. The Civil Rights and Equal Pay Acts passed in the 1960s had little or no effect on the broadcast or music industry as they applied to Blacks. Black women faced the double discrimination of race and gender. Although the owners of radio stations, advertising agencies and music companies promised to promote equality of opportunity in everything they do, they hardly ever did. Antidiscrimination laws have done nothing to level the playing field or improve the quality of life for most blacks in the entertainment field or in media.

In the industry, then and now, blacks, as one tenth of the population, were treated as inferior and were denied numerous civil rights, political rights and equal pay. Discrimination against black announcers and musicians became inherent.

In the few months after I arrived in the area, it was obvious that I had to do record hops and also make personal appearances if I were to maintain the standard of living that I wanted and was accustomed to. The money was good for Black deejays but nothing compared to the salaries of the whites. It was as if we were of a lower status and people of African decent had no desire for social mobility. It was evident that the white station owners and white record company executives knew that wealth meant power and prestige, and they were determined to keep it for themselves.

Some of the best times while a deejay at Katz was promoting shows and producing records of local artists. My first promotion occurred a couple of months after I arrived in St.Louis. In June 1965 I rented a former bowling alley located in East St. Louis and presented an old friend from Chicago, blues great McKinley Morganfield, known as "Muddy Waters". Muddy and I were neighbors in Chicago. He moved to Chicago in the late 1940's. He first recorded for Leonard and Phil Chess on the Aristocrat Label. They later formed Chess-Checker Records. His band included other friends of mine such as Little Walter on harp, and Jimmy Rogers on guitar. Some of my other friends were also part of Muddy's group, such as, Otis Spann, Junior Wells, Walter Horton, Leroy Foster, Big Crawford and James Cotton. I recorded two of my singles, 'Calling On My Buddies' and 'Soul Pearl' with Junior Wells' band for 4-Brother's Records.

The first show was a sellout and Muddy and I were quite happy. After this first show at the venue, the owner of the bowling alley converted it into a full time show club and named it 'The London House East'.

St. Louis had many nightclubs and bars in the African American community that featured live entertainment. One of the most admired entertainers in the area when I arrived was, bandleader, arranger, writer, producer and vocalist Oliver Sain. He produced and jumpstarted the careers of Fontella Bass,

Bobby McClure, The Sharpees, Uvee Hayes, The Montclair's, Shirley Brown, Barbara Carr, Ann Peebles and many more.

He and Ike Turner and Little Milton Campbell were long time friends and collaborators. Later he had several hits on his own as a vocalist, such as 'Bus Stop', 'Feel Like Dancing' and 'Soul Serenade'.

Another one was George Hudson's Band, highlighting Clark Terry and at one time featured Miles Davis, and some of the areas best male and female vocalists. Charles Drain was another popular singer and entertainer. He was the lead singer of The Tabs; Jules Carlos and the Bop-a-Deers; Bull and the Matadors; The Lamontes; The Smith Brothers; Gene Anderson and the International Hookup and countless more. The city was bustling with live entertainment.

BIG SIGNAL RADIO BROADCASTING CO. INC.
2733 BOMPART
ST. LOUIS, MISSOURI 63144
WO 1-1320 (314)

RICHARD J. MILLER
PRESIDENT

KXLW AIR PERSONALITIES

**PRESENTING RHYTHM AND BLUES, GOSPEL MUSIC, AND NEWS DAILY
AT 1320....ST. LOUIS, MISSOURI**

6 to 7 a.m.	LEONARD MORRIS....A pioneer of Gospel Music broadcasters in the St. Louis area. For 12 years, Leonard was the leading Gospel personality at KATZ, St. Louis. He is now a vital part of KXLW's Gospel Team, presenting the only daily Gospel Music in the St. Louis area.
7 to 9 a.m.	BERNIE HAYES....Graduate of the University of Illinois and veteran of the U.S. Air Force, he started his radio career with the Armed Forces Network. Since then, Bernie has been the featured R&B jock at several major stations before joining our staff at KXLW. Bernie's wit and great popularity is widespread throughout the community with both teens and adults.
9 to 10 a.m.	LEONARD MORRIS....
10 to 12 a.m.	COLUMBUS GREGORY....KXLW's Gospel Program Director has worked in the Gospel field for 15 years in the St. Louis area. Columbus has guided our Gospel Music programming with great success. He heads the team that penetrates the St. Louis area with the only daily Gospel Music voice.
12 to 2 p.m.	BERNIE HAYES....
2 to sign-off	STEVE BYRD....Steve attended Temple University, majoring in Radio & TV. Following his initial success with WDAS in Philadelphia, Steve came to KXLW. An immediate hit in St. Louis, this personable young man M.C.'s most of the touring top R&B shows appearing here. Without a doubt, Steve Byrd is King of the Scene with St. Louis teens.
NEWS DIRECTOR	AL "SCOOP" SANDERS....Who also serves as Director of all Public Affairs programming. Scoop's crisp, clear news delivery and his wide personal contacts within the community have won him recognition as the leading Negro newscaster in the St. Louis area.

The many clubs and lounges that did not feature live performers had to hire record spinners. That is how many of the radio personalities made extra cash to compensate for the low wages they were paid by their respective stations. With the long hours and the responsibility and obligation of hauling recording equipment and the latest recordings, the jobs were tedious and burdensome, and the pay was minimal, but every little bit helped. It was a time when the more popular you were with the public, the more you were in demand for record hops and emceeing programs.

In the mid 60's, as today, commercial radio stations used rating systems to measure the worth of personalities and programs. A station lived and died by the ratings. During this period, the most popular radio rating company in St. Louis was Pulse. They claimed to have developed a reliable procedure for obtaining accurate average half hour and cumulative audience data for radio. ARB (American Research Bureau) also entered the ratings war in St. Louis in 1967.

The method for gathering the data was through telephone calls to private homes. Those not-at-home for the original interview were supposedly contacted later. The problem was these companies did not call African Americans or other minorities, therefore the black stations hardly ever showed positively in the ratings game. And naturally with low ratings, the stations were unable to receive advertising dollars from the ad agencies, and consequently personalities were always under pressure to get 'better ratings'. It was a double-edged sword with both ends of the blade pointed toward the black deejay.

No matter what appeal we had in the community, the station owner had only one defining value and that was 'how much money can you make me?' While we were receiving accolades from our listeners and admirers, capitalist racial dynamics were still at play. We were still suffering discrimination because of our color and our race. There was compelling evidence of the strength of the black personality on the air, but we were still engaged in a vicious struggle for respect and parity from the owners; and a struggle for survival as an announcer. How do you balance these measures with respect for creativity and freedom of expression? The owners were always pursuing the advertising dollar regardless of its commitment to the public.

We were reaching our market, but we had no power to convince station management that we were the breadwinners for the facilities. All of the deejays complained about our conditions but no one would do or say anything. I decided that it was time for a change and it was up to me to better myself, and if possible, to make things better for my co-workers as well. We wanted decent pay, improved benefits and better working conditions.

In 1966, disappointed with the pay and compensation I was receiving from KATZ, I suggested to the other deejays that we should unionize. I was a member but on withdrawal from AFTRA (American Federation of Television and Radio Announcers) and IBEW (International Brotherhood of Electrical Worker's).

The American Federation of Television and Radio Artists unions consist of a group of local chapters that work together to improve wages and working conditions for its members. I thought this union was the one we should align ourselves with. The other association I suggested should be with IBEW. This amalgamation started in St. Louis in 1891 and was the union that the station engineers belonged, so I taught it would be ideal for us to be a part of. Organizing was our legal right and I convinced the others to organize and we chose AFTRA. We became members in the latter part of 1966, and from the day we joined, my days at KATZ were numbered. The same month we became members of the union, our salaries tripled, and our benefits increased. The deejays at that time were grateful and thankful of their decision to become union members. We felt we had achieved dignity, justice and most importantly solidarity.

CHAPTER 11

Westcott Distributors!

During this period the record industry was yet tremendously biased and in many ways, unconnected to the African American community. Mainstream radio stations and white record companies considered Black stations and artists substandard and backward, but not too inferior to keep white artists and white record companies from copying the black product. Even though the Black artists were selling to white fans, the main source of income was still going to white artists and their companies.

Discriminatory economic structure of the music industry has plagued African American for decades and some of my friends and I decided to act. We made a decision to open the first Black owned phonograph record distributorship in Missouri. In February 1966, Jim Taylor, Chuck Cunningham, Ted Hudson and I opened Westcott Record Distributors at 6843 Olive Street in University City, Missouri. I was elected president; Jimmy Taylor, vice-president; Ted Hudson, Treasurer and Chuck Cunningham, secretary.

Our thoughts were rooted in self-empowerment. We had visions and the energy, and we focused on creating positive changes in the record and distributing business.

We decided to model our operation after Ernie Leaner's United Record Distributors in Chicago. Ernie also owned One-Der-ful and Mar-V-Lus record labels. They owned "Do The 45" by the Sharpees, Alvin Cash's hit "Twine Time", the Five Dutones' "Shake a Tail Feather" and Otis Clay. My contacts as a deejay and my friends in Chicago made it easy for us to acquire most of the Black labels.

We were the exclusive regional distributors for specific labels and performers. These included Curtis Mayfield and Eddie Thomas' label Curtom; Duke-Peacock out of Houston; Bunky Sheppard's Labels; Vee-Jay and Constellation; Ruby Andrews; Nashville's Excello; Stan Lewis' Shreveport label Jewel;

Freeman Bosley's Teek Records; Ernie Leaner's One-der-ful and Mar-v-lus; and nearly every other Black owned label on the planet.

The R&B charts listed 'I Heard It Through The Grapevine—Gladys Knight & The Pips', 'Soul Man—Sam & Dave', 'Tell It Like It Is—Aaron Neville', 'Are You Lonely For Me—Freddie Scott', 'Make Me Yours—Bettye Swann', 'Respect—Aretha Franklin' 'Cold Sweat—James Brown', 'Higher And Higher—Jackie Wilson' and Get On Up—Esquires'. The local white distributors were outselling Westcott simply by sheer volume. They had more products with more hits on the charts. Of all the records I just named, Westcott distributed only the Esquires and Bettye Swann.

We were assertive businessmen and we were fair. Our prices were competitive and we alerted all of the small businesses and record stores of the deals the record companies were offering. We did not discriminate or play favorites, but we made sure the Black owners were competitive and treated with respect and their prices were as low as we could make them. We were successful, and with this success came the intimidation from the white distributors and storeowners. We were used to adversity and ready for the risks and whatever came with these risks.

The business was very profitable in the beginning, and we were providing jobs for local people and those who did business with us improved their profit margin. After a few months the other distributors and some of the white retailers began buying our product from their friends from out of state, a practice called 'trans-shipping'. Those who carried out this custom were able to buy our product below our cost and in return, they were able to sell our merchandise cheaper than we could. These retailers, some black and white would go to the dealers that were bootlegging our labels, rather than support us.

This routine was too much for some of my colleagues and in June 1967 I bought them out and ran the company on my own. I moved into a brand new unoccupied building at 2820 Delmar, near record row and designed the operation to accommodate the commercial action I was expecting.

I also had several offices built inside the building hoping to consolidate other black businesspersons who were involved in the music, record or radio industry. I wanted to make it a fundamental gathering place and provide accommodation for local businesses at a reasonable price. It was not long before Leo and Mamie Hutton moved into the building with me and opened Bamboo Records. They owned Mamie's Bamboo Lounge in St. Louis and wanted to get into the music recording business. They hired famous artist, writer and producer Andre 'Mr. Rhythm' Williams to run the company. Andre had worked for Motown Records and was noted as a prolific songwriter and performer. He had hit recording of "Bacon Fat", "Jailbait" and "Greasy Chicken", and he wrote "Shake A Tail Feather".

He produced hits for Jo Ann Garrett', Mel and Tim "Backfield In Motion" and 'Starting All Over Again', and Bull and the Matadors "The Funky Judge" while at Bamboo and achieved a distribution deal with Florence Greenberg's New York based Scepter-Wand Records. The label had R&B Artists Dionne Warwick, The Isley Brothers, Maxine Brown, The Esquires, Tommy Hunt, The Shirelles and Chuck Jackson, and several pop and doo-wop acts as well.

I was very happy with the success of Westcott. I was totally aware that the record industry thought that as long as they could control airplay and distribution outlets with large amounts of money, they could also control the market for their own profit. They never suspected that what they thought would have a negative impact would in fact motivate and encourage my desire to survive. I never entertained the thought of not achieving my objective or goals.

My promotional staff, including my brother John Hayes, Johnny Nance and Norma Jean Harrison, noted the preferences of our consumers and we extended sales locations. We diversified the distributing segment of the music industry supply network. Our customers began to shop in different African American locations for the sake of convenience, and we provided more selective soul music than the larger retail stores. People began looking in smaller specialized Mom and Pop stores that we serviced for what they needed.

During this same period, I was operating the Pageant Theater, presenting live shows by some of the most popular R&B singers and groups. The theater was located in the West End of St. Louis on Delmar near Hamilton. The Arthur Brothers, who also owned the Fox Theater in Midtown St. Louis, owned it, but I leased it from them and had complete control.

Some of the live acts that appeared at the Pageant are Patti Drew, Jerrio, Syl Johnson, The Sheppard's, The Impressions, Alvin Cash, Junior Walker, Donny Hathaway and Johnny Taylor. I kept the theater open for more than a year but the strain of being on the air, running a distributorship and producing records demanded too much time. I closed the theater and concentrated on broadcasting, producing and distributing.

In January 1968, after the continuous strain of trying to outmaneuver the other distributors, I began talking to Ernie Leaner about the possibility of merging Westcott and United Record Distributors. He was interested in the proposal so I began flying to Chicago nearly every weekend to work out the details and come up with a feasible plan that would be profitable for both parties and provide the best products for the cheapest price to our patrons. We had most of the fine points worked out and we were on our way to becoming a gigantic power in the music and distribution industry.

To finalize the merger, **April 4, 1968**, Ernie Leaner, William 'Bunky' Sheppard, George Leaner and George Williams flew to St. Louis for a meeting in my office. Just prior to signing the agreement, Andre Williams ran into my office and announced that **Dr. Martin Luther King had just been killed.** That immediately ended the meeting and the Chicago visitors right away headed back to the airport and returned home.

April 4, 1968 was a setback to the civil-rights movement and the beginning of the end of Westcott Distributors. The incident of that day ended the merger plans for me and essentially sealed the fate of the company. A few months later, I liquidated the business and concentrated on my radio and recording career.

By the end of 1966 and the first few months of 1967, I was constantly harassed and hassled by the local management team and from the absentee owners in New York. This came as no surprise. I expected the retaliation and the abuse for unionizing the facility. What I did not expect was extreme racism without any efforts for social justice.

In July 1967, I received a call from Richard R. Miller, the owner of KXLW, with an offer to join his staff at the daytime station. Daytime stations were broadcast facilities that operated from local sun-up to sundown. The talent there at the time was program director Al "Scoop Sanders" Gay; gospel announcer Leonard Morris; Steve Byrd; Hosea Gales and Columbus Gregory. I accepted the offer and after a two-week jaunt to New York, I retuned to begin two air shifts at the Brentwood facility. My first air shift was from 6 am until 10 am and the second air shift was from 2 pm until we signed off of the air. In the summer time it could be as late as 8:45 pm and in the winter months it could be as early as 4:30 pm.

Scoop Sanders was the principal cause of the success of KXLW. It was because of his leadership and foresight that the station achieved such prominence in the market. He was the news director and the production manager as well. He and I were the best of friends. I became god-father to his first born.

Leonard Morris and Bernie Hayes

At this point in time, I was pretty much establised as a popular announcer in the area. In the fall of 1967, Chicago music producer Jack Daniesl and John Barney asked me to compose, perform and record some original words penned by blues artist Junior Wells' "Up In Hear". Daniels and Barney owned Four Brothers Records and the only artist on the label was Tyrone Davis, who was at time called "Tyrone the Wonder Boy". I agreed to write and record the tune called 'Calling On My Buddies" and "The Soul Pearl". They were the first songs done in the style that was the precursor of what later became the genre known as rap music.The recording did well in St. Louis and across the country.

Scoop and I calobrated on several shows and other promotions. We did record hops together and our families socialized after work and on weekends. His pleasing personality and infectious smile was a trademark of this congenial broadcast professional. Our playlist reflected the music that was played and appreciated by our listeners

Leo Chears

I was under pressure from several sources during this time. The white record distributors were trying to persuade and influence Richard Miller, the owner of KXLW that being on the air and operating a record distributorship was a conflict of interest. I knew the law and I am sure they did, but this was a form of intimidation. The businessmen that operated the communications and record industry's were worried that the growing power of the Black record consumer and the expansion of Black owned record companies and radio stations would negatively impact their profits, and present more opportunities for minorities.

Miller and the others knew the truth but I was intimidated nevertheless. Scoop and I recognized the industry had lower expectations for minorities, and we took advantage of their failure to have appreciation for our collective knowledge of the business or our will to be successful. We produced the finest commercials, presented the best newscasts and played the most popular music.

Throughout this time, many notable talents passed through KXLW. Hank Spann joined us from Atlanta. Hank was a Chicagoan who migrated south and worked on several radio stations in the Southeast. Steve Byrd came in from Philadelphia. He was a Jimmy Bishop clone, and was a big hit, especially with the teen crowd. Shelly Pope was by far the choice of the adult set. Shelly had arrived from WNNR in New Orleans where he was the number one personality in the African American community. He attainted that status in the St. Louis area also, but he left the area after a year and returned to New Orleans.

Gentry Trotter was another talent associated with KXLW. Gentry produced several shows for the facility and was helpful in securing national advertising for the station.

Scoop and I continued to act as a team on many projects and promotions. We were the first to present the Jackson 5. We featured them on the East Side at the London House East. It was a memorable night because the Jackson's had run out of fuel and Scoop and I had to get them gas so they could make it to the gig.

We did a lot of shows and record hops also in Alton, and Godfrey Illinois. We were also dividing time doing air shifts at KADI, which was also owned by Dick Miller. KADI has an interesting history. The station at one time was a component of KADI twins—KADI FM and KADY AM. The AM is now KIRL, St. Charles.

KADI was located on the lower level of KXLW. Leo Cheers and George 'The G' Logan were sharing airtime with Ron 'Johnny Rabbit' Elz. It was a jazz station at that time and Scoop and I were part of the daily and weekend lineup.

Things began to change the latter part of 1968. Both Scoop and I somehow fell out of favor with Miller and we were accused of a variety of offenses that were either made up or concocted to intimidate us. We were used to challenging bigotry and prejudice, but this was something new. It seemed unprovoked and malicious. We decided the handwriting was on the wall as far as our future with Miller and we both began to seek other opportunities in the industry.

CHAPTER 12

Soul of the City-KWK

That good fortune came in early 1969 when Scoop was contacted by Bell Broadcasting of Detroit Michigan. Detroit dentists Dr. Haley Bell, Dr. Wendell Cox and Dr. Robert Bass owned Bell Broadcasting. The company had Detroit stations WHCB-AM and WCHD-FM and WJZZ. Dr. Bell had become the first black to build a station from the ground up. He constructed WCHB in Inkster, Michigan in the mid-50s.

Dr Wendell F. Cox was a 1944 graduate of Meharry Medical College. While tending to a flourishing dental practice in the Motor City, Dr. Cox leveraged his influence by purchasing broadcast properties that included WCHB and KWK.

The three doctors united with local businessmen John and Glennon Vatterott of St. Ann and Clifton W. Gates of St. Louis. They formed Vic-Way Broadcasting and applied for the frequency at 1380 AM that had been the historic **KWK** that was held by a temporary company, Radio 1380, Inc.

KWK had been off the air for years. On February 26, 1966 the FCC canceled the stations license after a fraudulent contest six years earlier, in 1960 relating to a treasure that was supposedly hidden in Tower Grove Park in St. Louis. Listeners complained to the Federal Communications Commission and it was revealed that the 'treasure' was placed in the hiding place only the day before a listener found it, even though clues to its location had been broadcast for several days before. Treasure seekers had already been to the location where the prize was found. KWK appealed, but the Supreme Court upheld the commission and awarded the frequency on an interim basis to Radio 1380, Inc.

The temporary or provisional operating license was issued to Vic-Way Broadcasting in 1969. We were hired to reopen and operate KWK 1380 AM. Scoop was hired as Program Director and I was selected as assistant PD and music director. Bell Broadcasting told us that we were hired for life.

The former transmitter was previously located at 500 Terminal Row, on Hall Street, on the bank of the Mississippi River, where most the motor freight terminals were situated. It was alleged that the previous owners did not want to sell to the new group and asked an unusually high price for the structure. The company decided to build a new tower at a new site on Chouteau Island, a few miles from the Hall street location off Interstate 270 and Illinois State Route 3. It took a few months for the engineers to get the signal phased in correctly but once it was done, the stations signal was one of the most powerful in the nation. One major problem with the transmitter's new location was the station frequently went off the air and sometimes remained off for days at a time. This was dreadful, particularly around rating periods. The station often had to send out of town for arts to repair the transmitter.

The offices were located in the Channel 30 Building at 12th and Cole in downtown St. Louis, but we broadcast from a trailer and a building at the 500 Terminal Row location. *I signed the station on the air at 5:00 am Monday morning, May 5, 1969.*

Scoop Sanders

Scoop and I were the only announcers for three days. We were known as '1380 KWK-The Soul of the City". Later in the week, Don St. John arrived and began his duties and later we hired Al Waples from KATZ and Decater Agnew. Mark Gordon-Meyers was our newscaster, and a few months later Donn Johnson and Ty (Thaxter) Wansley joined Lloyd DeCorley in the News Room. James Holt was our gospel deejay and Betty Thompson and Al Wallace hosted our public service programs. Soon, Bobby Knight and Gary "Tony" Stittum and Bill Bailey were added. Frank Davis headed the sales staff.

KWK immediately became the number one soul station in the St. Louis market. We were dedicated to providing the African American community and the community-at-large with the best programming available. We wanted to meet the needs of the young people without neglecting our adult listeners and respecting our elders. We knew the programming and the music were vital. We wanted to preserve the concept of personality radio and at the same time, present a balanced informational and entertaining source. We wanted to stimulate our listeners enjoyment and give them the awareness of their neighborhood. I wanted the station to be a stabilizing social function and a springboard to radio excellence.

The announcing staff and the office workers were as a family. We were oftend visited by the owners from Detroit. Dr. Bass visited more than the others. He often met with the local owners and spent days in the city at the stations offices downtown and the Hall Street studios. Scoop and I became very close friends with Dr. Bass. He was genuienly interested in the station and the well being of the staff. He made sure the payrolls were on time, and the sales staff had materials and the offices were adquately supplied.

ST. LOUIS, MO., THURS., MAY 11, 1972

KWK Off Air; Black Jocks Walk Out

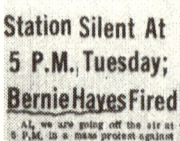

Station Silent At 5 P.M., Tuesday; Bernie Hayes Fired

Charles Gerber, national sales manager for Bell Broadcasting, was loaned to KWK from WCHB to add as many national spots as possible to increase the sales at KWK. The more sales would translate to higher revenue for the company. He would usually stay in the city for an entire week, returning to his family in Detroit on weekends. Gerber had connections with most of the adverstining agencies, both local and national. The new owners needed to buy new equiptment and update some of the existing apparatus.

KWK was a pioneer and originator of some of the customary practices in the industry today. We introduced long play album cuts and included them into the daily playlist lineup. Some songs as long as 15 minutes could be played at any time; and we would regularly play the other side of popular recordings. We were the first on most of the record company releases and we would not hesitate to air untested singles, albums or artists.

Another inovation was changing the speed of the recordings. We had a system of playing 45 rpm recordings at 50 rpm, and 33 1/3 recordings at 36 rpm. The increase in revoutions would make the recorings sound a little bit better on the air without distorting the resonance. The audience would not know the difference except to say our records sounded better than the other stations records.

We also promoted the station more with what little money we had. Our jingles were professional and good soundng. The station had time tones, and news introductions and weather jingles. We promoted a live show at an amuement park in North St. Louis in the Baden area that attracted more than tenthousand listeners. We also had a promotion in the Art Hill section of Forest Park that attracted nearly fifty-thousand.

Soon after establishing ourselves as a force in the marketplace, the owners hired Allan Eisenberg as general manager. He stayed only a few short months and soon left to accept the position as general sales manager for KATZ . Eisenberg also contributed to the demise of the art form that was Black radio. He knew very little about the African American community and even less about Black radio. The staff tolerated Eisenberg but we did not respect him as a manager or as a man.

Before long the local owners began fueding with the ansentee owners and eventually the two sides were far apart on strategy and direction of the station. Egoism and lack of consideration for others soon became an everyday event at the radio station. Tom Roper was hired as a sales manager and he would tell the Detroit owners eveything that transpired locally, therby dividing the union even more. Dr. Cox would frequently come to town and upset and denigrate the entire staff, and eventually created such a disturbance that the office staff and the air personnell threated to leave the facility.

A letter to the FCC, alledgedly written by Allan Eisenberg, accused Scoop and me of receiving payola from record promoters and recording companies. That alledgely held up the issuance of the broadcast license to the owners. Scoop and I went to the FCC and to a hearing in Newark, New Jersey to defend ourselves of the false allegations and the license was awarded to Vic-Way Broadcasting on May 5, 1972. Not too long after the issuance of the license, the St. Louis faction and the Detroit group parted ways. The Detroit group finally wrestled control from the St. Louis partnership.

Scoop left the radio station to accept a job as the weatherman on KTVI-channel 2, the ABC affiliate in the city. That left the job of operating and programming the station to me. During this period, the St. Louis music scene was reflecting the national changes introduced and implemented by the conglomerates. Major labels were signing black artist. I was also recording during this time also, and Jim Gates and I had gained immense popularity in the area with our television dance and variety show on Channel 30.

Our first TV show was 'The Black Circle Hour' and later we developed the "Soul Brotherhood Show". I recorded four recordings for Volt Records, a sister label to Stax. Wendell Cox, insinuating a conflict of interest also used this against me. He wanted to take full control of programming and acted as a micro-manager of the facility from Detroit.

On May 6, 1972, only one day after the FCC issued KWK its license, Cox brought in two white men from Tennessee to program and operate the station. He appointed Joseph McDermott as program director and operations manager, and Al Greenfield as the general manager. McDermott took an air shift using the name Mac Allen.

The two had programmed a station in Memphis and other southern cities. . They immediately changed the play list from R&B to a pop and top 40 oriented record list. The intent was to slowly turn the station to a general market facility and abandon the African American market.

The announcers and office staff resented the proposed changes, especially the idea that the African American community would again be shortchanged, and we were insulted because the owners suggested that there were no qualified Black people capable of programming and operating the facility. When the two white programmers attended a meeting with Cox and Bell in Detroit, on May 9, 1972 the announcer and staff walked out of KWK. When the executives in Detroit heard about the action, they flew into town for a series of meetings. Meanwhile, the community and several civil rights and social organizations joined our ranks and formed picket lines around the offices and studios. CORE, The Congress of Racial Equality lead the other activist and aided in the negotiations.

Our requests were simple. We wanted the station to remain dedicated to the African American community. Scoop, Donn St. John, Donn Johnson and I had researched trans-cultural practices in music and broadcasting, and we knew the value of adapting and adjusting policies to meet our target audience.

We knew suffering from discrimination, be it race, national origin, religion, sex, age and even sexual orientation. We had all suffered and we were not about to become part of the problem instead of the solution. The demonstrations went on for nearly a month, until finally there was a settlement the second week of June.

I was reinstated as program director, music director and operations manager, and everyone else returned to their respective jobs and duties. Naturally after this campaign, I realized my days were numbered at the station regardless of the promises of no retaliation. We again became the number one soul station in the region.

In the early 70's, the Black personality deejay was again a vanishing breed. More of the white owned and several of the black owned broadcasting companies were insisting that new formats must be the tool for presenting culture on radio, but they were failing to say 'White Culture'. Fewer live remotes and fewer newscasts were implemented on more and more stations, and less restrictive legislation was passed by the FCC, allowing some of the white deejays to get away with language that was never permitted or acceptable otherwise. The traditional concept of radio was obsolete according to the efficiency experts. But we knew the community you serve must reflect its function; it must also be entertaining and informative. I knew in order to achieve this; we must compete with other stations that are in the traditional pop vein and with stations that were programming a more moderate form of Black Music. We incorporated politics, record reviews and interviews with local personalities and national recording artists. We became even more visible in the marketplace, emceeing shows and promoting live acts as well as doing record hops.

Our Black competitors were suffering the same fate as the White stations that ignored our audiences, by not taking into account the interests of listeners. They were more interested in the advertising agencies and of the industries financing radio, thus neglecting radio's true values and leading to a general decline in listeners. Some others Black music formats changed to alternative rock, and some to a more easy listening, soft adult contemporary format. The radio formats became less diverse, but we at KWK began tracking the varying tastes and shifting demographics of our listeners.

Most of the stations at the time were programmed to a broad target audience. The competition was fierce and each station was fighting for a share of the advertising dollar. KMOX, the CBS owned 50,000-watt clear channel station always got the biggest piece of the pie. Next the top 40 and pop general market stations would get buys and the African American stations were always last if they were bought at all. This is another factor that convinced many Black owners to try attempting to appeal to the white listener, and dropping the 'personality' that sounded Black. Many adopted an all gospel or religious format.

We stayed true to the people who supported us because we had an obligation to expose people to the music they loved and bought. We wanted to satisfy our core listeners while attracting new listeners with the very best programming possible. Even though the advertising agencies knew that we attracted young, white, middle-class listeners, the rating services never admitted it nor did they reflect theses facts in their systems. We yet survived. Frank Davis and I would travel to other cities at our expense to make presentations to advertising agencies, hoping to keep the station on the air. And with all of this devotion and commitment, the owners of KWK nearly abandoned the facility and left us more often than not, to provide for ourselves.

In the fall of 1972, Harvey Lynch was hired as general manager. He had recently managed a station in Memphis, Tennessee and had sold himself on the Detroit executives, convincing them that he could boost ratings and increase profits for the station. Lynch immediately fired most of the deejays and brought in Tom Joyner, Jake Jordan and Sonny Joe White. The deejays that remained were Tony Stittum, Decater Agnew and Jim Gates. I remained as Program Director and Frank Davis continued as Sales Manager. The station moved from the trailers of Hall Street to the Mansion House Center in Downtown St. Louis.

Lynch considered himself a wheeler-dealer and was not trusted by any of the previous staff members. These doubts and suspicions of Lynch proved to be true when he once again, arbitrary fired more staff members and caused more distrust among the workers. Finally he replaced me as PD with Jim Gates and made Agnew the music director. I realized later that this was the retaliatory plan of Wendell Cox for my actions against the station. It did not matter because I had previously auditioned for an announcer's position and weather forecasting position at KTVI-Channel 2, the ABC affiliate in St. Louis, to replace Scoop Sanders who had taken a TV anchors job in Baltimore.

I left KWK in September 1972 and accepted the position at KTVI—TV. My choice was the correct one because in 1973, less than a year later, the station closed and was placed in receivership.

While working at Channel 2, I was still involved with local radio, and aware of the trends and movements of the genre. Early in 1972, I was hired by the Anhueser-Busch Company to market a new product. In 971 Budweiser Malt Liquor was introduced to the marketplace. August A. Busch, Jr. named chief executive officer and I was hired as the African American spokesman for BUDWEISER MALT LIQUOR. The brewery sponsored 'The Bernie Hayes Show', a three-hour jazz program, from Midnight until Three, Monday through Friday on KATZ, funded exclusively for Bud Malt Liquor.

The show lasted for 26 weeks, and I was shuffling my duties between the television station and the radio station. I never stopped assessing the changes that were occurring in the media. I noticed more and more Black stations folding or changing formats. Some companies changed to moderate conversions and some to gospel or religious formats.

The white or top 40 music stations were not generous when it came to playing Black music. Of the top 10 albums of 1972 only two African American artists were listed. Curtis Mayfield and Roberta Flack were included in the list that included Carole King, Don McLean, Neil Young, America, Jethro Tull, The Rolling Stones, Elton John, Cat Stevens and Moody Blues.

In 1973, only Diana Ross made the top 40 music stations in most industry trade publications.. That list was comprised of Carly Simon, War, Elton John, Eric Wiessberg, Alice Cooper, Pink Floyd, Elvis Presley, Led Zeppelin, The Beatles, Paul McCartney, George Harrison, Chicago and Jethro Tull.

The Ojay's, Eddie Kendricks, Gladys Knight and the Pips, Roberta Flack, Diana Ross, Marvin Gaye, Billy Preston and Stevie Wonder were the only single Black crossover artists that were consistently on the top 40 charts. This again reflected the struggle smaller Black labels were facing, and African American artists were systematically being kept out of the so-called mainstream and off of the pop music charts.

These are the practices that were so pervasive during the 60's and 70's that initiated the change in so many Black formats that eventually led to the casting out of African American personalities.

Metropolitan areas tend to enjoy a wide number of formats, but Black radio stations categories were constantly changing. The primary purpose of this was to keep the music separate. It is another form of segregation, implicating that African American music formats were isolated from the pop, country, and classical and other styles.

Remember, the early Black music was classified as Race music; that evolved to R&B and Soul; then came Black, and then Urban, and Urban Contemporary with sub-categories of hip-hop, rap and house music, and gospel and now contemporary gospel.

Most areas will have several different stations to choose from. White audiences could choose from top 40, Rock, Rhythmic Oldies, Nostalgia, Hot Adult Contemporary, Easy Listening, Country, Classical, Classic Rock, Classical Hits, Christian Contemporary, Alternative, Adult Contemporary, and Adult Albums.

Blacks have Blues, Jazz, Gospel, Hip Hop, Urban and Oldies. They even separate these. Rhythmic Oldies signify White Oldies and Oldies mean Black Oldies. Christian Contemporary is White Christian and Gospel relates to

Black. From its roots to the modern age, Black music and Black oriented radio stations have been kept in an inferior grouping.

Some types have crossover appeal, such as News and Talk, Sports and Smooth Jazz. Public and Community radio stations also have mass interests. These examples illustrate the importance of people of color responding to the changes in the industry. One of the most preposterous terms I heard remarked by some black programmers and some Black stations was that some considered some Black artists and some Black Music *TOO BLACK*, and refused to play anything that did not sound like what some programmers considered void of the ethnic black resonance. That further reduced the outlets for Black artists and Black entertainers, and further made me lose confidence in some African American communication specialists.

The white stations focused on a segment of the market that they considered important, and ignored the other segments, thereby promoting the disparity and segregation of Black consumers and Black listeners.

The same developments that challenged the radio and recording industries in the early days emerged into the marketplace in the 60's and 70's. The businesses never considered the rights and needs of the minorities that kept them in production. Their motivation was then as it is now, pure greed. And while white America was constantly connecting to their ethnic heritage, white radio stations and most black radio stations treated the blues as dysfunctional and a bastard form of degenerative music. Most whites in the early days through the early 70's, disregarded the art form, despite the widespread acceptance by Black people. Not until the materialization of FM, and the exposure on community and college radio stations was the blues revealed to thousands of white people.

Music was the primary influence that attracted listeners to Black radio stations. News and sports occupied just a small percentage of the broadcast day and the focus was on the most hits one could play in any given hour. By accepting such an arrangement the Black community was always playing catch up to activities that were occurring in the society. Politics, educational issues and other minority problems and topics were often never mentioned, but social functions such as concerts, shows and other forms of entertainment were promoted. Black newspapers, usually published weekly, were usually the main source of news for the Black community, except for some announcements in church bulletins and religious publications.

One of the best documentaries on the Black Press is a PBS documentary called '*The Black Press-Soldiers Without Sword*'. Bill Moyers said '*Soldiers Without Swords" retrieves an important missing page from American history and brings it virtually to life. It's beautifully produced and directed and tells a story as only a powerful film can do."*

The Black Newspapers in St. Louis included The St. Louis American, The St. Louis Argus and The St. Louis Sentinel.

The oldest Black Owned newspaper and the oldest Black Owned business in Missouri is the St. Louis Argus, founded in 1912 by Joseph and William Mitchell. The first issue of the *St. Louis American*, the second black-owned newspaper in St. Louis, appeared on March 17, 1928. In 1928, Nathan B. Young co-founded the *St. Louis American*, for which he served as publisher and editorial writer for more than forty-three years. The late Howard B. Woods founded the St. Louis Metro Sentinel in 1968. Wood's also started a weekly radio broadcast on radio station WTMV, now WESL-AM. On the other side of the Mississippi, the East St. Louis Monitor, a weekly some time ago ran by Clyde Jordan, was the main source of information for the African American community.

While Black radio news was a vital component during the Civil Rights and Black Power struggles of the 60's, the priorities had shifted after Black folks thought the movement had produced better opportunities and a brighter future for all. Meanwhile the number of Black owned radio stations were decreasing. Black people were again suffering from the loss of some of the most valued and important resources they had.

In the early to middle 70's, another style of music was introduced to the masses that influenced a lot of Black radio stations. Disco, a combination of Black Soul and British Funk got the nation dancing. Blacks and whites embraced the new genre and once again the African American community was caught between a rock and a hard place. Some Black stations altered their record lists to incorporate the new form, while some others changed their music formats completely. Whereas some remained dedicated to Rhythm and Blues and added perhaps the top disco records to their lists.

Van McCoy had a hit with "The Hustle", "Love's Theme", by Love Unlimited Orchestra was added to nearly all of the play lists of R&B and most Black oriented stations. Then other stations, both AM and FM initiated changes that reflected the popular music. But disco was not new. It was originally called discotheque music and was very popular in clubs played by local record spinners.

Some Soul performers who were early to recognize the trend and recorded songs that became disco hits include "I'll Make Me a Man" by Barbara Acklin, "If You Love Me Like You Say You Love Me" by Betty Wright, "Zing! Went the Strings of My Heart" by the Trammps, "This is the House Where Love Died" by First Choice, and two by Eddie Kendricks, "Date with the Rain" and "Girl, You Need a Change of Mind".

Donna Summer's "Love to love you baby, "The Love I Lost" by Harold Melvin and the Blue Notes, "Rock the Boat" by the Hues Corporation and 'Theme From Shaft' by Isaac Hayes were big hits on mostly all stations, both black and white, and eventually nearly all of the major labels were releasing disco singles and albums.

KC & The Sunshine Band, Earth Wind & Fire, Hot Chocolate, Kool & The Gang, and The Trammps had hits, and "Fly Robin Fly" by Silver Convention was another huge hit. Disco lasted well through the 70's, and the movies helped to accelerate the movement with "Saturday Night Fever", starring John Travolta dancing to the music of Bee Gees.

Disco was the forerunner of some of today's music, such as hip-hop, House, Rap, and pop. It was another nail in the coffin of the demise of Black personality radio. New recording artists as well as veterans in the business were frantically trying to get a disco hit. The performers were signing with new labels, and some of the older, more established artists were seeking new contracts. Record labels were certainly essential for the success of any artist, and the purpose of any new artists or band was reaching an agreement with a label.

Various singers and musicians were so anxious to sign a contract with a record company that they often gave up royalties and rights they were due.

The music companies often invested a lot of time and money in new talent and consequently the record companies would not give a true account of the royalties. Most veterans knew the procedures and often negotiated their contract through their attorneys. Many acts merely used their recordings for exposure to acquire personal appearance engagements.

In the 60' and 70's, while some Black stations were adapting to more moderate and contemporary music formats, and installing computers to replace live bodies, the Small Business Administration started a program that made the purchase of radio stations more accessible to minorities. Minority Enterprise Small Business Investment Companies or MESBIC's. These were privately owned and managed investment firms mandated to provide equity capital and debt relief to new, small independent businesses. Criteria for investment and size and type of investment vary from one firm to another.

1977

JIM (Gentleman Jim) GATES
4 p.m. to 7 p.m.

MICHAEL (Mike) KEY
7 p.m. to 9 p.m.

CHARLES (Sweet Charlie) SMITH
6 a.m. to 10 a.m.

WESL 1490 RADIO

THE BEST IN BLACK

EAST ST. LOUIS, ILLINOIS

EARL RUSSELL
Account Executive

MICHAEL BROOKS
Account Executive

BILL (Fox Chaser) MOORE
12 Midnight to 3 a.m.

ROD KING
9 p.m. to 12 Midnight

TOM (Shot Gun) PAYNE
1 p.m. to 4 p.m.

Black owned WESL play list

The aid also included federally guaranteed loans and government-sponsored management and technical assistance, and although several Black men and women used MESBICs to buy stations, many of them abandoned the more contemporary urban formats, and adopted fast paced, top 40 sounding programming.

Though the MESBIC enabled many minority entrepreneurs to form new businesses, the results were disappointing, because of the lack of administrative experience, poor locations, and shortages of funds led to high failure rates. These minority businesses faced considerably risk in terms of location and market instability, and in some cases, lack of community response to certain programming styles.

Even though radio revolutionized communication many years ago, the African American market never truly got its fair share or proper recognition. The higher positions on the dial and lower power, kept the signals poor and the profits low. The Federal Communications Commission assigned FM (frequency modulation) ninety channels between 88 and 106 megacycles, twenty of which, from 88 to 92 megacycles, are for non-commercial educational FM. The AM band, that most Black stations operated, extended from 550-1600 kHz, with the Black stations usually at the far right, at the lowest point of power.

In 1974, while at KTVI-Channel 2, I accepted a deejay position in the evening at WESL-1490 AM in East St. Louis, Illinois. It was still considered a personality radio station with some of the areas most popular announcers. I joined Jim Gates, Doug Eason, Curtis "Soul" Brown, Frank Davis, Charles 'Sweet Charlie" Smith and Michael Tyrone Key.

Although there was a station play list, the music structure was pretty loose and there was never a problem getting any records played. The drawback was the station was licensed for 1000 watts but operating on less than 500 watts. The stations signal was limited to a very small listening audience, and the competition from KATZ made it difficult to obtain advertising from the agencies. The rating surveys literally ignored the facility, so the deejays relied on personal appearances to supplement their low salaries. The format remained dedicated to soul and R&B music, but having such a low profile in the marketplace, we were not able to influence any changes or raise any ethical or social changes. The station became another vehicle for music and entertainment and nothing else.

While the mainstream media was rapidly expanding, Black oriented radio stations seemed stuck in a rut that did not allow them to become more progressive. But this was merely a perception. Actually, it was the decision of black programmers not knowing or caring about their history or heritage, and disregarded the responsibility to the people they served. New technology and increasing competition demanded that urban stations track audience behavior and respond to the needs of the community, but in many instances, this point was overlooked and many outlets continued to struggle.

Black radio announcers had an oral tradition of informing the community of vital news and services important to their community, but with a new generation of programmers, their focus was on purely entertainment and profit. This is not a conflict because commercial stations exist on their margin of profit, but in many ways, they could have become wealthy, entertained and enriched their listeners and served the community interest. There are many ways to program to hold an audience's interest and present cultural programs, but too many chose not to do so. Thus, another needed breath lost from Black radio.

CHAPTER 13

Blaxploitation Movies Genre!

In 1971, Melvin Van Peebles introduced the nation and the world to a new genre in moviemaking. He wrote, directed and produced **"Sweet Sweetback's Baadasssss Song".** This was an experience that startled the theater going public. The style was called blaxexploitation, and later shortened to Blaxploitation. It was proclaimed as the advent of a new era in Hollywood and for blacks in film. It kicked off a method, or movement that was soon imitated by most of the major studios. It broke the pattern of black depiction in feature films and opened doors for black producers, writers and actors. It cast young black men and women as young black revolutionaries who fought the white establishment and won. Suddenly a new crop of Black super-heroes and heroines appeared and the cinema industry experienced a sudden recovery, thanks to the films. The pictures created some positive images as well as some negative stereotypes.

The character and influence of these movies evolved with the civil rights and black power movements, and developed into another media culture and transformed some peoples' personal lives. The movies boosted a slowing economy and saved many faltering movies studios. Hollywood's financial troubles were widespread and it was a segment of the population that was once barred form the industry that found them once again exploited, but at the same time, rescuers. White movie directors, producers and writers gained tremendously from the African American culture and talent of the exploited. It was good for black actors who were out of work, although some were unconvinced.

I believe that some of the youths that emulated some of the stars of Blaxploitation movies became the parents of some of the youths that became some of the nations most violent. A few of the movies that I believe had a negative impact on Black culture and destroyed lives and limbs were 'Superfly' starring Ron O'Neal, Carl Lee, Sheila Frazier; The Mack' with Max Julien, Don Gordon, and Richard Pryor; 'Across 110th Street' starring Yaphet Kotto, Anthony Quinn, Tony Franciosa; 'Black Mama, White Mama' with Pam Grier and Shelly Winters; 'Dolemite' with Rudy Ray Moore, D'Urville Martin, Jerry Jones; 'Black

Belt Jones' starring Jim Kelly, Gloria Hendry, Scatman Crothers; 'Black Caesar' with a cast of Fred (The Hammer) Williamson, Gloria Hendry, Julius W. Harris and 'Shaft' starring Richard Roundtree, Moses Gunn, Charles Cioffi..

There were many more that I and others considered harmful and destructive, and I consider a forerunner of the 'gangsta rap' and hip-hop genre.

CHAPTER 14

KKSS-Stereo In Black!

Times were changing rapidly in Black radio. A lot of FM stations began courting the African American market and the black stations started their own crossover experience, by playing more white and pop music. They called it "Urban Contemporary," with its "more music, less talk" theory, as I earlier described, and they began to woo white advertisers and national advertising agencies. A few African American owners were fortunate enough to purchase some stations in major markets, but it was exceptional when they did. The media empires had already begun to manipulate the industry. They controlled multiple communications outlets and were on a path of domination.

In April 1975, I obtained the opportunity to create a format that I had desired for many years. The Amaturo Group, headed by Joe Amaturo of Fort Lauderdale, Florida, bought St. Louis Adult Contemporary FM station KGRV from Intermedia, Inc. of Kansas City. Missouri. KGRV was a 100, 000 watt class A FM station, located at 1215 Cole Street in downtown St. Louis, in the Channel 30 building. We began operations on April 9, 1975.

The station had a great signal that covered the entire St. Louis metropolitan area. Alan Eisenberg was named General Manager and Donnie Brooks was brought in from New Orleans as program director and I was hired as a deejay and assistant program director. Our goal was to convert the Adult Contemporary format to a more up to date urban style and hire local African American celebrities who were already established in the market.

I was assigned to the early morning wakeup show. Scott St. James, a white announcer and hold over from the previous owners, was the mid-morning deejay; Donnie Brooks held down the afternoon drive position; Robert 'Scotty Lawrence' Salter was the evening personality and Gary 'Starr' Perks was the overnight announcer. Carole Carper was hired as the newsperson and community affairs director. Gary Perks died in 1985.

I personally wanted to inform as well as entertain our listeners by giving them a comprehensive overview of the areas that concerned them. They should know of new laws, and what is happening at City Hall, and news and changes in their ward politics. I did not want to make it a talk or information program, but these topics could be inserted between records and presented as public service announcements. The information was offered in a clear and informative style, fused with lively entertaining chatter.

The music list was typical rhythm and blues with a smattering of top 40 or white crossover recordings. After a month on the air, Donnie Brooks left for a weekend visit to New Orleans and stayed for nearly a month. I took over his duties while he was away. After another week, Eisenberg decided to replace Donnie and offered me the position of program director and operations manager. I declined until I spoke with Donnie who told me he decided to remain in New Orleans, and he insisted that I accept the offer and I did. Donnie Brooks passed in November 2003.

I immediately instituted some new programming ideas and added the music that I thought would compliment our listeners and earn a respectable market share for our owners. I combined the most popular soul records and oldies with modern and contemporary jazz and disco by both white and black artists. The innovation was an instant success and we had both black and whites in nearly equal numbers. I also initiated a Black History Calendar that told our listeners what happened on that particular day in African American history. We also covered and announced local social and civic events.

Because of their exposure in various media, the announcers at the station were chosen to host most of the concerts as well as church events and legislative social functions. The station was far more successful that anyone could have hoped for.

Within the next few months more local superstars joined our staff. Veterans such as Lou 'Fatha' Thimes, John Gardner and Johnny Jones were all well known and respected in the area, having worked at other local radio and television stations. The staff was one of the best in the country.

Eisenberg contracted with New York Deejay and personality Frankie Crocker to arrange our logo and signature jingles. They were the same he used at WBLS-FM in New York.

In heavy echo, the recorded jingle announced "KKSS-Stereo in Black-107 point 9-In Stereo". The call letters would 'bounce' one after the other in separate channels. In other words, the first letter 'K' would be in the left channel only on your stereo speaker, and the next letter K would be in the right channel. It was the same array for each 'S'. It was a very distinctive sound that set us apart from others in the market.

With the station gaining such popularity, I was contacted by the St. Louis American Newspaper to write a column about the music and entertainment industry. The St Louis American Newspaper is one of the oldest African-American publications. It began in 1928 and is recognized as one of the nations leading newspapers, regardless of ethnicity.

I wrote about local and national recording artists, and general news about the communications business. The column was a hit in the community and I received several awards for its content and worth. I also wrote about and promoted KKSS radio.

After a few months, Eisenberg wanted Frankie Crocker to program KKSS from WBLS because of Crocker's success in the New York market. Crocker's general-market afternoon radio show was No. 1 with New York City with audiences 12-and-over, and 18-34 in some time slots.

Crocker wanted to turn the KKSS music list into a mix of eighty percent disco and Salsa music. He would prepare the play list from New York and send it to us in St. Louis. I objected when Eisenberg suggested the practice, but Eisenberg carried out the plan. I opposed the arrangement because I knew the St. Louis market would not support such a mix as Crocker planned because St. Louis was not a pure disco market, and certainly our listeners were not supporters of the music. I knew and the other announcers knew that this was a move that would sink the station.

I was also apprehensive of accepting Crocker's list because of allegations of payola associated with the music that he programmed at his station. I had been through a similar situation with KWK and I did not want even the impression of impropriety associated with the KKSS music list.

Crocker had been indicted in Newark on charges of lying before a federal grand jury investigating allegations of payola in the recording industry, when he denied receiving money from record companies to promote their records. He was found guilty, but the verdict was later reversed. I did not want or need the hassle.

Immediately after introducing Crocker's music, the listeners began to complain by telephone and by mail. I called Crocker and explained to him and to Eisenberg that the St. Louis area did not have the number of Hispanics and Latinos as New York. My argument did not convince them but they gave me authorization to replace some of Crocker's disco and salsa songs with choices of my own. I evaluated our market and created a list that indicated the top selling and most popular songs in the area. I eventually regained nearly the entire play list and once again our numbers climbed. Our Arbitron ratings jumped from number 12 to number 5, making us one of the most popular radio stations in the area.

In January 1977, because KKSS was so successful, Alan Eisenberg decided it was time to abandon the Black market and program to attract more white listeners and gradually become a general market station. I was not at all surprised because Eisenberg had sent me a memo instructing me and the other announcers to stop announcing from the Black History Calendar. The memo read 'enough of that Black stuff'-do away with the calendar'. I was disturbed and disappointed by the memorandum but I complied.

In order to implement this plan, on March 1, 1977, Eisenberg selected the stations only white announcer, Scott St. James to program KKSS, and remove me from my time slot and appoint me as community affairs director. I objected to the changes first and foremost because I knew that St. James knew nothing about programming, especially to the African American community, a fact, which he personally admitted. The staff also realized that this was a terrible decision and they expressed their views to Eisenberg. The objections went unheeded and Eisenberg made his move.

During this period, it was revealed that Scott St. James, a white announcer and my subordinate, was making more than a hundred dollars a week more than I was making. His salary was always more than Donnie Brooks and mine from the day we started broadcasting at KKSS.

I asked Eisenberg why was St. James' salary higher than mine and he said 'White people are used to making more money than Black people'. I was disappointed by his answer but not surprised.

The local community immediately protested the changes at KKSS and several demonstrations and picket lines were formed in front of the station. The February 17, 1977 issue of the St. Louis Argus Newspaper, columnist Red Wilford wrote about the changes at KKSS and the community uproar, Wilford wrote 'Black Radio Is On Its Way Out: 'Black Culture-Black Pride-Black Heritage has just received its first kick'. The daily St. Louis Globe Democrat and the St. Louis Post Dispatch carried stories in their papers, and the Black weekly's, The Argus, The St. Louis American and the St. Louis Sentinel as well as community newspapers such as the Jeff-Van-Der-Lou, reported on the events in relation to the actions at KKSS. Within a week, the community had initiated a boycott of KKSS.

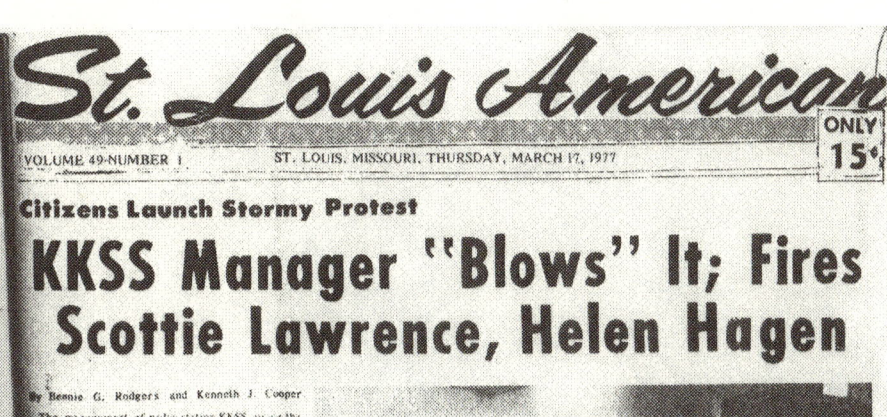

St. Louis American

VOLUME 49-NUMBER 1   ST. LOUIS, MISSOURI, THURSDAY, MARCH 17, 1977   ONLY 15¢

Citizens Launch Stormy Protest

KKSS Manager "Blows" It; Fires Scottie Lawrence, Helen Hagen

By Bernie G. Rodgers and Kenneth J. Cooper

The management of radio station KKSS, using the tactics of the white bosses who sought reprisals against blacks who challenged status quo and used the late Dr. Martin Luther King in his Montgomery, Ala. demonstrations, last Friday dismissed one of its "superstars" and a female disc jockey who had likely been called "the first black female disc jockey" in St. Louis.

The victims of the "reprisals" caused by protests that grew out of dissatisfaction at the station over the demotion of Bernie Hayes and the elevation of a white disc jockey, were Scottie Lawrence, better known as medical surgery as pharm...

St. Louis American

VOLUME 48-NUMBER 50   ST. LOUIS, MISSOURI, THURSDAY, FEBRUARY 24, 1977

No Kissin' At KKSS

"Stereo In Black" Station Grooms White Man For Managing Position

BY MARTHA RABER

"What's going on at the station is apparent to everyone except Johnnie Jones. Every black at KKSS has been discriminated against. Now they have replaced Bernie Hayes with a black who doesn't know what's going on and created a position for Scott St. James," asserts Karl Banks, a former account executive with KKSS radio.

Last week it was announced that popular disc jockey, Bernie Hayes had been replaced as the station's program director by Johnnie Jones. Hayes had been KKSS' program director, musical director and operations manager; he is now relieved of those duties in order to become community affairs director, a new title but a demotion, friends of Hayes' have told the American. Scott St. James, a white, is replacing Hayes as musical director and also taking over Hayes' morning show.

Shifts in the KKSS program schedule were explained to the American by station manager Alan Eisenberg, who said that the arrival of Helen Hagan, whom he said will be the first black female D. J. in the area, necessitated the change. Hagan will take over the 1:00 p. m. to 4:00 p. m. show formerly

hosted by St. James. Eisenberg emphasized the importance of Hayes' community affairs position. "We are trying to enhance our relations and service to the community," he said. "Bernie will be able to get out into the community more."

"If they are so interested in community affairs, why did they change the news from Mutual Black Radio to ABC?" asks Arlene Martin, a former employee. "There were many calls and letters in favor of the black news show, but the final answer comes from Eisenberg and money!" Martin agreed with other sources that there is across the board discrimination at KKSS. "Eisenberg has been doing this since day one," she said. "It's nothing new. He runs the place by plantation rule—the 'overseer' beats whomever he wants to." Martin charged that although more blacks than whites are employed by KKSS, the whites make twice as much money in most cases.

One observer very close to the situation told the American that Eisenberg is expected to move to a station in Texas owned by the Amaturo Group, which also owns KKSS. The observer further stated that

Continued on Page 13

Alan Eisenberg

Bernie Hayes

Meanwhile, on March 21st, I filed a racial discrimination grievance with the EEOC (Equal Employment Opportunity Commission) regarding the pay disparity in pay between St. James and me. Immediately after filing the complaint, Johnny Jones was appointed program director and I was demoted and assigned the midnight shift. I began receiving harassing memoranda from Eisenberg and Jones, with the intent of forcing me to resign. The local community was now applying pressure to the station to reinstate me to my former positions. Petitions were circulated charging the stations owner with blatant acts of racism, and asserting that KKSS had slapped the Black community in the face, and demanded the removal of Scott St. James and Alan Eisenberg. More than ten thousand signatures were gathered on the petitions and sent to the Federal Communications Commission with copies to the owner, Joseph Amaturo.

Johnny Jones was ostracized in the public's eye for standing with St. James and Eisenberg and turning his back on the people who once supported him and the station. St. James left under the pressure and Jones assumed his duties as well. Subsequent to the actions of the community, Scotty Lawrence, whose real name is Robert Salter, and I was fired, along with Helen Hagen who had just been hired from Philadelphia, Pennsylvania for the mid-morning slot.

Our firings created an upheaval among the protesters and our supporters and eventually Amaturo came to town in an attempt to calm the community and salvage what he could of his station and former sponsors. The boycott had taken its toll and revenue to the station had dropped tremendously. It was evident that the station was in dire strain, and the community's actions were successful.

In June, 1977 I was hired by Wendell Bates to be the Midwest Regional Promotions and Marketing Manager for MCA Record Company. I did not return to the airways of KKSS.

On January 20, 1978, I received my right to sue letter from the St. Louis Commission on Human Rights and I proceeded with the racial discrimination lawsuit against KKSS and the Amaturo Group. In May 1978, the racial discrimination suit was settled in my favor. A few weeks later, Alan Eisenberg was fired.

The owners changed the call letters of KKSS; misleading the community into thinking the station was no longer operating. It was a ploy to fool the public and it worked. In 1979, the station switched to an urban format and the call letters changed from KKSS and became KMJM-FM Majic 108. It is now Majic 105.

CHAPTER 15

MCA Records!

In 1977, after several attempts to gain a foothold in the R&B market, Wendell Bates convinced MCA Records, to add a separate marketing division and concentrate on that specific sector. I was hired as the Midwest Promotional and Marketing Manager.

MCA has a long and diverse history. Dr. Jules Stein founded The Music Corporation of America (MCA) in Chicago in 1924 as a talent agency. In 1958 MCA purchased the Universal Movie Studios back lot for 11 million dollars, and they obtained a portion of The Paramount Pictures film annals for MCA's TV division.

In 1962 MCA merged with Universal Pictures, and they in addition bought Decca Records. Lew Wasserman became president of MCA. In 1966 MCA started **UNI Records**, and signed Olivia Newton John and Elton John to record deals. The label had several pop and country artists and delved slightly into but never penetrated the Soul or R&B market. Hosea 'Make Me a Hero' Wilson was the national promotional director for the Black Music Division, and George "C" Chavous was the assistant for the division. The Black artists were Hugh Masekela, Lovelace Watkins, The Lovelites and Big Black. They had some success with moderate hits with Betty Everett's 'There'll Come A Time', and 'Jealous Kind of Fella' by Garland Green. The label folded in 1973.

When Bates assembled his team in 1977, the black music division became a major force in the development and marketing of black artists. The first promotional staff consisted of Lamont Simpkins—Atlanta; Sparkle Kemp-L.A.; Earl Sellers-New York. Each person was responsible for a region of the country I was responsible for the Midwest from my base in St. Louis.

My area included Kansas City Missouri with the oldest Black Owned station West of the Mississippi River, KPRS. Mr. Skip Carter opened KPRS-AM in May 1950. In 1963 the Carter's were granted a licenses for a 100, 000 watts FM facility and KPRS—AM and FM simulcast the same programs.

1979 MCA promotional staff

During my tenure, Skips' son Michael, also named Skip, and his daughter, Prim, managed the station. The AM facility changed their call letter to KPRT and the FM retained the KPRS identification. They were the highest rated stations in the area. The AM eventually changed to an all gospel format and the FM played R&B.

The MCA pop music division had established performers such as Elton John, Olivia Newton John, The Who and Neal Sedaka. The Black music division started off with Peaches and Herb, Anacostia, War, Rose Royce and Al Hudson and the Soul Partners. We struggled for airplay for a while and in the spring of 1979 I was offered a comparable Midwest promotional position by Mike Abbott with ABC Records, which I accepted, because the artists' roster was like a who's who among R&B talent. ABC Records distributed Dot, Dunhill, Duke, Impulse, Paramount, and Duke-Peacock labels.

The roster included B.B. King, Bobby Bland, Ray Charles, Marilyn McCoo and Billy Davis, Dobie Gray, Chaka Kahn, The Dramatics, The Crusaders, Randi Crawford, and many more, along with Peaches and Herb, War, Rose Royce and Al Hudson and the Soul Partners. I was very happy with the new position but after three months with ABC, the company was sold to MCA Records for twenty million dollars and I returned to the very same position that I had left, but with greater product to work. I was happy to be with old friends again.

Wendell Bates was no longer heading the MCA Black Music Division. Bates started an independent promotional company and stayed on the West Coast to build his business. Mike Abbott was now in charge of MCA's Black Music pro-motions and he relocated the entire ABC crew to MCA. I returned to my University City offices and the other members remained in their respective cities. With improved product and more recognition, it was a lot easier getting records on the air.

There were disadvantages being Black promotion personnel in a large white owned corporate giant like MCA. Because we were issued credit cards and air-line cards, the company comptrollers wanted a receipt for every payout on our expense account. This only became a problem when you treated some Black deejays to lunch or dinner. Most of the places we frequented did not give receipts. Most soul food restaurants and BBQ restaurants at that time did not issue receipts and when we listed these costs on our expense reports, we were usually denied repayment. This always caused a problem and consequently, we lost a lot of money. The other divisions did not have these problems because their clients usually dined in first class, upscale dinning rooms and cafes.

Another problem was the unfairness because of lack of assistance for the Black Music Division. We produced a significant and important amount of revenue for the company but we received only a pittance in field support. We were never allowed the same level of monies or support as the white music divisions. When it came to the R&B division, MCA was not evenhanded when it came to reciprocity. Our division always came up short.

During this period, the music industry made Rock and Roll and Pop music into an international discourse, while attempting to leave Rhythm and Blues and black independent labels behind. There was technological change and cul-tural and style changes as well. The British rockers had made their impact and Motown had established a distinct sound as had Chicago and Memphis in the soul markets, but the majors yet wanted to control and limit Blacks artists and black labels. Major performers were still struggling to get their fair share of a market that was large enough for all.

Our new staff at MCA incorporated some of the most interesting and orig-inal minds in the industry. We had the best product, the most recognized and respected artists and proven hit material. In spite of everything mentioned, the white stations and some urban stations resisted our efforts and made it quite difficult to have our records auditioned or reviewed. We expected this resist-ance from the general market stations, but when black businesses adopted the same policy as the white stations we were perplexed. This was another example of Blacks imitating whites and hoping they will be treated as whites. It never works, nor will it ever. These stations for the most part did not receive any spe-cial treatment from record companies or advertising agencies. It was the same old story of the slave trying to please the master.

The roots of the soul sound had been established early in the 20's and through its evolution the contributions were beyond compare. Yet the medium called radio still kept this genre relegated to a second-class form, nearly always segregated from the so-called main or majority charts or general public. The role of black Americans in the evolution of popular music went virtually ignored. Only a few black and white stations appreciated the struggle from which this music evolved and gave it the exposure it deserved. It was not until the materialization of FM, college and community radio stations that the art form gained true and well-deserved recognition and a semblance of fair or equal play. Some actually explored the dimensions of this music on cultural change, intellectual development and human interaction.

The Midwest Region included St. Louis, Chicago, Milwaukee, Cincinnati, Indianapolis, Louisville, Pittsburgh, Cleveland, Detroit, Kansas City, Omaha, Des Moines and Minneapolis—St. Paul. While I was the regional promotions director with offices in each city I also had a local promotional person who worked their respective city or metropolitan area on a daily basis. Our jobs included getting airplay for our artists, but it also included artist collaboration and teamwork, concert corroboration, in store displays and general marketing in department store and other retail outlets.

Lawrence Hilton-Jacobs, Bernie Hayes,
Chicago dee- jay and Chuck Barksdale of the Dells

We were responsible for providing tickets to radio and television personnel for local concerts or artists appearances; setting press conferences when appropriate and securing venues for performance and for sleeping arrangements for events that required overnight stays and travel. We were the true driving force behind MCA records in the late 70's but we were treated as stepchildren.

Some of the most memorable occurrences at MCA was our charge to promote the black oriented films our parent company, Universal Pictures, had produced. We had the soundtrack to the movies and we were assigned the task of accompanying each film to the major cities in our market for special showings and promotions, often with the stars of the movies.

Universal Pictures was founded in 1912. In 1915 Universal City Studios moved onto the world's largest studio lot. In 1946 the company merged with International Pictures and in 1952 finally sold Universal International to Decca Records. In 1962 Lew Wasserman of MCA bought Universal and started the first made-for-television movie series and set up the Universal City studio tours.

'Car Wash', starred Richard Pryor, Franklin Ajaye and Ivan Dixon featured the Pointer Sisters. It was a big hit for Universal and MCA records. Rose Royce did the soundtrack.

'Which Way is Up?' is a comedy starring Richard Pryor and Lonette McGhee. Pryor plays three roles. 'A Woman Called Moses' starred Cicely Tyson as Harriet Tubman. It also starred Robert Hooks and was narrated by Orson Wells.

The most significant of the films and the one that the company really banked on was 'The Wiz''. This movie was the African American version of the Wizard of Oz. The movie starred Diana Ross, Michael Jackson, Richard Pryor, Nipsey Russell, Lena Horne, Ted Ross, Mabel King Thelma Carpenter and Theresa Merrit. Quincy Jones performed the soundtrack, and this was a huge hit among Black people but whites did not support the movie in the theaters and Universal considered it a failure at the box office.

We all loved it and the venues where we presented the feature received raving revues from the viewers. It was again a matter of culture and a division in basic cultural perception. I thought it was the usual response of white people to the omnipresent racism of that period. In this vast field of film commentary, the company yet did not want to accept the opinions of their Black audiences, despite the breadth of research evidence we provided, the company decided it was not worthy of an advertising or promotional campaign to attract white audiences.

The MCA years were to me a landmark achievement into the minds and actions of the corporate world of the music business. I further understood that regardless of ones history, culture, legends and folklore, the company was only interested in the bottom line. They wanted to sell, sell and sell. Black entertainers in the twentieth century faced hardships, prejudice and cultural barriers, yet they aspired to fulfill their dreams and cultivate visions. We had a saying about the record business; 'it's hard but it's fair'. This was partly true. It is very hard, but it is certainly not fair. I left MCA Records in March 1979 and returned to KATZ radio in St. Louis.

CHAPTER 16

Another Concept!

In 1979 Doug Eason was general manager at KATZ. He hired me to do overnights at the station and allowed me to plan what I thought would be a different approach to all night programming. I cherished the opportunity to present to an audience what I thought was unique and distinctive. I remembered the songs and artists that had been popular in the late 50's and 60's through the middle 70's but were almost ignored on the oldies lists. Artists that had only one or two hits, and records that became popular but more or less disappeared from the charts.

I resurrected some of these treasures and the public received them with reverence. The show became a real success. Another notion that I instituted was presenting the most popular singers or groups in what I termed a *'mini-concert'*, meaning that I presented nothing but those artists for an entire segment of the program. After that model was established, I would feature one artist or group against the other, such as the Temptations versus the Miracles. The listeners loved the idea and I decided to actually call some of the artists live on the telephone and let them speak to their all night listeners. After three month of the all night show I was assigned to the early morning wake up spot. I thought it would be a good idea to also speak to some of the entertainers to let our listeners know that these performers considered the entertainment industry 'a business', and that it should be recognized and treated as a business. I got permission for Doug Eason to allot a portion of the morning show to a combination of music and talk.

Some of the first persons I called included Jerry Butler, Dick Gregory, Luther Ingram, Muhammad Ali, Curtis Mayfield and others. Soon I began talking to the mayor, the Governor and other politicians and soon the show was all talk. Minister Louis Farrakhan of the Nation of Islam and Imam Warith Dean Muhammad of the American Muslim Mission were frequent quests. It was the first talk show and call in program for the African American community and it was a huge success.

Almost immediately after the call in portion of the program became known, I started receiving complaints about city services, police brutality, political issues and educational concerns. In 1979, although the residents of St. Louis were half of the population, the mayor, the police chief and the superintendent of schools were white. I asked the community why? If the people were half of the population of a city, why were they not equally represented? The questions excited the community and soon there were campaigns to elect a black mayor, a black police chief and a black school superintendent.

Early in 1981, Dr. Jerome B. Jones was selected as Superintendent of St. Louis Public Schools. It was a first for the city and I felt very good having been the one that instilled the thought into the populace. I was happy that the listeners comprehended the need for a leader that had concern for their children's future. I provided Dr. Jones and the St. Louis Public Schools an hour every other week on the morning talk show.

In 1993 Freeman R. Bosley Jr. was elected Mayor of St. Louis. Bosley was the first African American to hold the office.

Bosley was a graduate from Central High School and Saint Louis University. He earned degrees in Urban Affairs and Political Science and received his J.D. from Saint Louis University Law School in 1979. While a student at St. Louis University, Bosley was president of the Black Student Alliance and the Black-American Law students Association. Bosley was the first African-American St. Louis Circuit Clerk for the 22nd Judicial Circuit—a position he has held for 10 years. He served as the 3rd Ward Democratic Committeeman, chairman of the St. Louis City Democratic Central Association, and the first African-American chairman of the Democratic Party.

Bosley's father, Freeman R. Bosley, Sr., is a city alderman from the 3rd Ward. His grandfather, Preston Bosley, was the son of a slave who established the Yeatman Community Development Corp. and Yeatman Community Health Center.

In 1991 Clarence Harmon became the city's first African-American police chief. Harmon advanced from detective to police chief in 21 years. He later succeeded Bosley as Mayor. I felt that I played a significant part in these gentlemen acquiring these offices. I am very proud to say that I was emotionally fulfilled.

I am sure that the talk radio program also added to the end of the genre known as Black radio. Soon several other black formatted AM stations began to add talk to their schedules. Some limited talk to the weekends while others added the design to their daily schedules.

Jack Gibson featured my talk show in his magazine "Jack The Rapper", and suggested that this would be the style for AM radio stations in the future. He also suggested to radio AM and some FM stations that were financially failing or struggling in certain markets to adopt a talk format. He revealed how successful my program had become and many stations in other markets followed the lead. 'Jack the Rapper' or 'Mello Yello' as it was sometimes referred to, was started by Gibson in 1976, and was the first Black music trade publication. It was the journal that industry professionals respected and followed as far as new music releases; news of performers and producers; market trends and inside news about black radio and black television.

Because of the success of my program, I called one of my closest friends, Pervis Spann at WVON in Chicago and tried to convince him to change his daily format to all talk. He and Wesley South were familiar with talk radio because South was considered the father of Chicago talk radio. He started Wesley South's Hotline in 1962 and it was the most listened to talk show in the city. He preceded Spann's midnight blues show in the early 60's after the Chess brothers bought WVON. Pervis did not take my advice until a few years later when he became owner of the station. It later became the talk giant it is today.

After Gibson highlighted the achievements and activities of my show in St. Louis, I began to receive inquires from other stations and announcers. Also, more black news departments began to network with others and me around the country. The reports were getting out and more and more were embracing the design. With the change, many owners, black and white, began to interpret and understand the impact of the social and economic status of African American families by listening to those who called talk radio shows. The popularity of the programs challenged the common assumption that people wanted only music on AM and FM stations.

While most music companies attempt to manipulate market with over saturation of certain artist's products, talk radio would endeavor to service the community with news and entertainment without any hidden messages. From the beginning, my talk show gave an authentic and comprehensive picture of the community in addition to national events, and allowed my listeners to give their views and opinions on issues that either concerned them or affected them. We addressed topics of importance to the public and offered recommended positive approaches to solve our problems. I tried to make the world's first mass broadcast medium a forum for positive change.

As disk jockeys we often challenged bigotry and unfairness, but a talk show could reach not only our neighborhood, but also mainstream American culture. Yet, the general market stations and most R&B stations had no sense of duty or commitment. The beat went on and on. They never placed local needs above ratings or commercial interests. The landscape was closing in on local personalities and the outlook was gloomy.

In 1981 I thought the political and economic fabric of American domestic life was in jeopardy. More music categories were creeping in and no one in the music business could figure out what the trend for the 1980s was going to be. There was Adult Contemporary, AOR, Classic Rock, Alternative Rock, Hard Rock, Metal, Country, Bluegrass, Folk, Broadway, Christian, Gospel, Disco, Dance, Opera, Pop, New Age, and at the lower end of the spectrum was Jazz, R&B, Hip-Hop, Rap and Blues. Lionel Richie's duet with Diana Ross was a crossover hit, but again, the industry did not want to bridge the cultural divide, nor did they want to confront the dilemmas of a changing American culture. Thus, the music charts were treated as Holy Scripture and no one seemed ready to challenge the titans of the industry. There was a silent revolution and black radio and the black music industry was suffering.

Record sales were down and the trend revealed they would continue to decline, so record companies began producing videos to promote a new album, and the price of singles rose dramatically. This is the year that the first compact discs appeared in the marketplace, and the Walkman cassette players were household items. This phenomenon struck another blow to Black music oriented stations and small record labels that were already suffering. The industry was again feeding on those who could least support it, and that continues to reverberate today.

It was evident that white station owners who programmed to the African American community had devised strategies to fool their audiences by acting as if to be concerned about the problems of these persons. It was then as it is now, simple to find black people who do not feel a kinship to their community. These people are the program directors and music directors, primarily in northern cities, who will mislead their followers into believing that the stations cares about them, while the working classes and the poorer listeners are duped into believing theses Judas' with black faces.

The integrity that was once associated with the term 'black radio' was ignored by this new generation of black announcers, programmers and their owners. They were not interested in reflecting or influencing Black culture, or establishing camaraderie with the persons they were licensed to serve. They were only interested in manipulating the truth, entertaining and keeping the public ignorant of politics and educational development. They abuse the trust and the system.

By the 1970s such abuses of the system by commercial owners, program directors and politicians, the die was cast that radio as we knew it was nearly obsolete. It was if management forgot to understand the relationship between broadcasters and the public. They focused only the economic aspects of the business. I wanted to broaden the understanding and discussion of the obligation that broadcasts companies' hold. They seemed to have not remembered.

Another occurrence that contributed to the destruction of the radio, as we knew it, was the FCC reversing its position on broadcast regulations. The FCC substantially reduced the burdens on broadcasters with its Deregulation of Radio in 1981. According to official federal documents, the FCC eliminated "guidelines" indicating how much informational programming each station should carry to have its license renewed, replacing it with "a generalized obligation for commercial radio stations to offer programming responsive to public issues, and abolition of FCC guidelines on maximum commercial time allowed on radio stations." This in effect gave the stations a way out. They were no longer 'obligated' to provide the community with scarcely any public service information while simultaneously allowing the stations to increase their commercial segments. They were also excused from providing any formal documentation of "community needs".

No entertainment guidelines required AM stations to offer 8 percent of entertainment programming and FM stations to offer 6 percent. News, informational programs, talk, and public affairs were considered non-entertainment; while entertainment programming consisted of music.

The stations were once required to have 'ascertainment' meetings with the public, which was a process required to gather input from the community. The process was to determine issues of importance to their listeners and to then provide evidence of the station's response to those concerns. The stations were also limited to no more than 18 minutes of commercial announcements per hour.

The 1981 deregulation was total market reform and it meant a devastating change in the way the radio business accomplished. It was a blow to the public that would only start a downhill spiral of greed and deceit. It provided in my view, a license to steal and further ignore the public trust and commitment. Owners who never cared about their obligation were now able to renew their license without impunity. The public interest was ignored.

While the industry should have been addressing the issue of fairness and diversity, deregulation was changing the media landscape. The lawmakers had lost their perspective and neglected to consider the negative impact these changes would have on minority ownership. They failed to realize that FCC deregulation did not support or promote diversity of entertainment programming. It was if they completely abandoned their awareness of moral or ethical decisions. The media is supposed to provide an important source of information, and not cater to the rich and powerful.

The Black Music scene was changing in the middle 80's. Except in the South, most R&B stations were programming tunes that they hoped would attract a huge number of white listeners. One such artist that received a lot of attention was Anita Baker. Her 1983 album **SONGSTRESS** opened doors for her and other black artists. The hip-hop genre along with Rap was also catching on with white listeners and the Black stations almost deserted their traditional black audiences and concentrated on appealing to the masses.

These new rap and hip-hop performers did not care about proper grammar, usage or style of the English language, nor did they care about criticism or condemnation of their verbal style. Soon the denigration of women slithered into the music and it was nearly all down hill from there. Some artists attempted to weave a positive spin into the music, but never expressing the importance of strong language skills. One such group was Two Live Crew who was notorious for their graphic lyrics. The group was arrested in Miami for performing what law enforcement considered obscene material. Two Live Crew was vindicated when The Supreme Court decided that the group was performing and exerting their First Amendment rights that guaranteed them freedom of speech.

The words 'Nigga' and 'Niggaz', and the term 'Gangsta Rap' appeared more frequently in trade magazines, and on record labels, and soon they became the norm in hip-hop culture and with all of the undermining mistakes and illogical transitions, there was no concentrated out cry from academia. The music became almost dehumanizing and stereotypical. In terms of treatment of women, the lyrics to some tunes glorified violence, sexual exploitation and lewd lifestyles. These recordings mostly portrayed male domination, but soon several women and a number of female groups were portraying the same promiscuous behavior, both in the content of their music and from their actions during live performances. There was little difference between pop or hip-hop culture and obscenity. The lifestyle of young adults, both black and white and their elders was growing exceeding apart. It was a subtle separation, but nevertheless, a significant division.

Parents began to notice that their teenagers were wearing sagging pants down near their knees and oversized clothes. The masses noticed that urban culture did not only impress their musical taste, but children's attitudes were changing. Rappers were proud that their music had an effect on people's actions and deed, although some denied some negative actions associated with the music. Most urban rappers claimed that their music reflected life in their neighborhoods, but this was mostly bunk. It was an expected, perfectly defensible answer, but in many cases it was not true. The fact that some of the music promoted violence and murder irritated some police organizations and some peace and civil rights advocates.

Steve Allen and Charlton Heston and several other national entertainers headed groups including some religious organizations that lobbied Congress and record companies to censor certain lyrics of Rap performers that these persons deemed offensive and wanted in some instances, laws passed to restrict or punish the artists and their companies that released what these persons referred to as objectionable and offensive. Congress did pass laws that more or less controlled lyrics, by mandating a labeling system that prevented lyrics containing violence and profanity being sold to children. There is no evidence that the process worked, although the lawmakers and record company executives insists that it does.

The genre also encourages and glamorizes fortune and expensive flashy clothes, expensive cars and often, promiscuous usually light skinned women. Some women's groups lobbied against the images portrayed by women and some radio stations joined forces to keep the filth off the air. But to some this was another form of censorship, and to others, it was a biased act against black artists.

Some organizations sought to ban music and videos that they considered obscene and indecent, but the Federal Communications Commission is explicit in their rules and regulations. Regarding obscene and indecent content, the FCC states: 'it is a violation of federal law to broadcast obscene programming at any time. It is also a violation of federal law to broadcast indecent programming during certain hours. Congress has given the Federal Communications Commission (FCC) the responsibility for administratively enforcing the law that governs these types of broadcasts.

The Commission may revoke a station license, impose a monetary forfeiture, or issue a warning, for the broadcast of obscene or indecent material.' The commission also stress that 'Obscene speech is not protected by the First Amendment and cannot be broadcast at any time. To be obscene, material must meet a three-prong test'. An average person, applying contemporary community standards, must find that the material, as a whole, appeals to the prurient interest; The material must depict or describe, in a patently offensive way, sexual conduct specifically defined by applicable law; and (3) The material, taken as a whole, must lack serious literary, artistic, political, or scientific value.

According to the commissions website: 'The FCC has defined broadcast indecency as "language or material that, in context, depicts or describes, in terms patently offensive as measured by contemporary community broadcast standards for the broadcast medium, sexual or excretory organs or activities." Indecent programming contains patently offensive sexual or excretory references that do not rise to the level of obscenity. As such, the courts have held that indecent material is protected by the First Amendment and cannot be banned entirely. It may, however, be restricted in order to avoid its broadcast during times of the day when there is a reasonable risk that children may be in the audience'.

It was simple to recognize that the government and media owners did not focus on the structure, conduct or performance of the industry, but only the profit the owners could gather and the favors some commissioners and industry professional could receive. The diversity and regulation of ownership was a non-issue. Media monopoly was now the motivation of the agency and the rich owners of radio, television and print corporations. Federal indecency rules bar the broadcast of obscene material and limit the airing of material that contains sexual or excretory references in a patently offensive manner to late-night hours when children are less likely to be watching. During the 8:30-9 p.m.

The Federal Communications Commission with its chairman Michael K. Powell embarked on an investigation into the 2004 controversial Super Bowl halftime show. The exposure of singer Janet Jackson's breast and the sexualized dance routine precipitating it Powell asserted, violated indecency standards set in law and enforced by the Commission.

In February 2004, radio shock jock Howard Stern was fired by Clear Channel Radio, the U.S.'s largest radio chain for not "conforming to acceptable standards of responsible broadcasting", and for indecent content. Stern was accused by the station of conduct "vulgar, offensive and insulting, not just to women and African-Americans but to anyone with a sense of common decency."

Through 1985 I was the most listened to African American radio personality in the St. Louis area. Phil Donahue and Oprah Winfrey were the undisputed leaders in daytime television talk programming, starting in the early 80's. In 1983 Sally Jessy Raphael began broadcasting a celebrity talk show in St. Louis. By 1985, Sally had become nationally syndicated and became a prime player in the national talk show genre. Throughout this period, my local radio talk show was the most provocative and provided more local information and discussed diverse topics than the previously mentioned programs.

It was a trying time because although the listeners wanted information, station management and some local politicians and power brokers did not want the public to become too informed. One station manager did all in her power to shut me up and made life miserable for me at the facility. She tried to prevent me from emceeing public programs and she did not want me to accept any awards. This was finally exposed through Eric Mink's column in the St. Louis Post Dispatch Newspaper.

Locally and nationally elected public officials also wanted to keep some of their deeds and activities away from the public's eye. When some of their dealings were exposed they wanted to shut the program down, but the audience would not allow it. The public organized and picketed the station and ultimately the general manager was replaced and my program was secure. Many positive changes occurred after the demonstrations.

I would feature local and national figures from all walks of life. I kept some of the original contributors from 1979 and added an assortment of interesting, stimulating guest that would talk about subjects that were of interest to my audience. Another regular feature of the program were the recorded audio-tapes or live interviews with the nations leading Afrocentric scholars that I aired at specific times. Recordings of Malcolm X, Dr. Martin Luther King and live sessions with Dr. John Henrick Clarke, Molefi Kete Asante, Yosef ben-Jochannan, Dr. Maulana Karenga, Jacob H. Carruthers, Dr. Bruce Bridges, Dr. Asa Hilliard, Brother Charles Finch, Marimba Ani, Dr. Leonard Jeffries, Jr., Tony Martin, Theophile Obenga and others.

These intellectuals contributed so much to our program through their extensive cultural studies and their connection to the global society stimulated our listeners to activism and brought so many into consciousness of their history and many other topics worldwide. Their mix of political radicalism and debate provoked our audience to support local and national candidates in elections and got the public involved in the struggles of South Africa and others communities in the African Diaspora.

CHAPTER 17

The Mississippi Experience!

In March 1985, after becoming totally disgusted with the Black electorate of St. Louis, I moved to my wife's home near Macon, Mississippi, the county seat of Noxubee County, located approximately 35 miles south of Columbus, Mississippi and about 15 miles West of the Alabama state line. I was dismayed because the citizens of St. Louis had the opportunity to elect a Black Mayor for the City of St. Louis and the majority of Black voters stayed home. They let a golden opportunity pass them by and I was absolutely embarrassed by this lack of action by so many that had bragged about their power and their willingness to assert it. I felt that I was wasting my time trying to educate and inform the people of the region. As a result I moved to Mississippi.

Reecy L. Dickson, my wife's sister was the Superintendent of Education for Noxubee County. She was the first Black elected official of that county since Reconstruction, and she was a forceful community leader. My wife and I decided to move south and attempt to forget the frustrations of the big city. I landed a job as a television reporter at WCBI-TV, a CBS affiliate in Columbus. Columbus is located on the Tennessee-Tombigbee River and is the home of Mississippi University for Women, Columbus Air Force Base, and the first home of playwright Tennessee Williams. I was a general assignment reporter, covering the counties of Noxubee, Clay, Lowndes and Winston, and occasionally traveling to Attalla. I never stopped loving radio and yearning to return to the airway while keeping up with the trends in the medium.

I listened to local rhythm and blues stations in Columbus and West Point, Mississippi and a couple of stations located in nearby Alabama. The main difference that I noticed about these small local stations compared to the larger markets such as Memphis, St. Louis, Chicago and even Jackson, Mississippi was the local deejays, both men and women had nearly abandoned typical black sounding material and opted for a more general marketed hip-hop type format. Most of the announcers were either in their late teens or early twenties. They had no concept of real personality radio and connection to the music of their forerunners. Only Jackson and smaller cities with radio stations generally under a thousand watts would occasionally play a true blues or R&B record. Sadly enough, theses stations were a microcosm of most of the black oriented stations all over the country. They had abandoned their rich African-American culture for what they were told was a new movement and a finer direction for young Black children, while they were only serving a selfish money hungry market that cared nothing about them.

I promoted a few shows while I worked in Mississippi just to stay in the frame of mind of the entertainment and communication media. I presented Bobby "Blue" Bland and Bobby Rush at various times, but I was surprised that locals in the area either did not listen to the area radio stations to learn that these Black acts were appearing or they did not believe they would actually be appearing live and in person at the local venues. At one performance in Macon, several persons insisted that Bobby Rush was not Bobby Rush simply because of the location he was playing. It was disheartening but I had to accept the reality of the issue. People had allowed their heritage to slip away and without a fight. Long hard years of struggle by Black deejays, artists, producers, writers, promoters and owners seemed to be shattered.

BOBBY "BLUE" BLAND
Duke Recording Artist

Exclusively booked by:
BUFFALO BOOKING AGENCY

The radio stations in Columbus and West Point, Mississippi were considered the leaders in Black programming but the music was directed entirely to the teen market. The Deejays were considered personalities because each projected a separate and unique identity, some with slogans and personal theme songs. But the music was the same as any other soul station copying white formats. Actually the black artists played on these stations were carbon copies of white acts except for the established soul performers from established Black labels. Companies such as Motown, Atlantic, Stax, Malaco, Arista and a few others, along with the few independent labels on the play lists were the only ties these stations had to the community they were meant to serve. Most had abandoned any resemblance to what Black people considered Black formatted stations.

Also, there were no talk or informational oriented programs directed to the African American community. There was no pretense of caring about the community, or examining the conditions of how their listeners existed. It was another failure of the system that we once called personality radio, good radio in general. Information is crucially important to the survival of a people but the majority of the Black radio stations that I listened to from St. Louis, to Memphis, to Jackson, Mississippi to the Alabama and Louisiana borders concentrated only on entertainment that was absolutely of no importance to their audience.

The culture of political transition through information to better the quality of life for the populace was ignored. Black people were still at the mercy of the sons and daughters of previous slave owners and the Black people running the local stations were as much to blame as anyone. They had no idea of the critically important issues of the day that their listeners were not receiving. Black radio was in a far worse state in the middle 80s than they were during the peak of the civil rights struggles. Very few Black announcers or program directors chose personal missions to unearth the truth and deliver it to their listeners.

During this period I had become totally disgusted with what I had perceived as the New South. It was the same ole south, without the overt Jim Crow traditions, in most places. The illusion of a new way of life and new opportunities for people of color was only a dream. Although some minorities benefited by more liberal standards imposed by federal and state governments, the majority of the citizens still suffered from the legacy of Jim Crow and White Supremacists ideology.

The banks owned most of the land that was once owned by blacks, and the commercial businesses were nearly all white owned. Black farmers were discriminated against and denied access to most federal, state and local programs designed to help their kind. Black urban residents, who usually made up the majority of the population, did not have access to county hospitals and other municipal services that their tax monies should have guaranteed. Usually they did not have a voice in such matters and rarely did they attend city or county council meetings. They were not included in the University's outreach programs and were discouraged from attending agricultural meetings where the latest updates in the industry were discussed. It was overwhelming to me. Where I once thought was a more relaxing and productive way of life turned out to be just another illusion and a case of wishful thinking. I had experienced enough.

Early in 1987, I began talking to several radio stations in St. Louis. I spoke with Bill White, a pioneer who led the fight for a radio station in St Louis and the owner of KIRL-1460 AM radio in St. Charles, Missouri. Bill had run for Congress against congressman William Clay but lost the contest. He was now running the radio station full time, with his wife Virginia. He offered me an announcer's position.

I also spoke with Tom Lewis, a friend from high school. He and James J. Hutchinson owned Inter-Urban Broadcasting and had purchased KATZ-1600 AM in St. Louis. Tom also asked me to return to St. Louis and host another talk and music show. I accepted the offer.

I also spoke with William 'Bunky' Sheppard, one of my best friends from the music industry, who was now living in New Orleans, about relocating back to the Gateway to the West, or to some other locale. Bunky, previously an independent producer in Chicago, was an executive at Vee Jay Records and the discoverer of Gene Chandler, the "Duke of Earl", The Esquires, the Sheppard's, The Dukay's and many others. He was also a previous owner, along with Ewart Abner of Constellation Records.

While discussing my desire to leave Mississippi, Bunky cut a few minor hits on my wife, Uvee Hayes. Bunky had collaborated with Jerry Butler, Brenda Lee Eager and others over the years and had access to several potential hit tunes at his disposal. He arranged for several sessions in New Orleans, Detroit, Cleveland and Memphis to record Uvee, using such musicians' as Stevie Wonder, The Phoenix Horns and Jerry Butler among others. The records were moderate hits in Chicago, Baltimore, and St. Louis, the Carolina's and other places around the nation.

The local stations were playing from the Billboard charts and the trend in Black music was even more divided by the categories black artists were allowing themselves to be placed in. To further the profits of white record companies and retailers, it was necessary to position these recordings in a separate section in order to make the performers believe they were receiving special attention. It was a ploy to segregate them and keep them happy, and put an end to the potential for competitiveness in the marketplace, and cross-cultural assimilation. With the lack of sales of product specifically targeted to the African American community, the artists and black music companies promotes an ethos of failure and social stigma.

Black music types were: Classic R&B and Soul; Gospel; Modern R&B; Northern Soul-Philly Soul; Southern Soul-Stax.

The style of black music and the artists were rapidly changing from a Black sound to a more generic fashion. For example, the Isley Brothers' hit in 1985 was 'Caravan of Love' by Isley-Jasper-Isley; there was Debarge, Kool and the Gang; Rene and Angela; Frankie Beverly; Freddie Jackson and the Temptations had a mellow sound for their release of 'treat Her Like A Lady'. The music was not R&B or Soul anymore. It was a black form of what white radio had always been.

With the success of a few recordings, and a track record to build on, and the promise of a job from Tom Lewis, I resigned from WCBI-TV and left Mississippi.

CHAPTER 18

The Return to the Midwest Jungle!

In the fall of 1987, we returned to St. Louis where I was to begin work at KATZ. When I arrived in the city, I was informed that the position that I was promised had been given to Mildred Gaddis. Mildred had been the news director and talk show host on Magic 108 FM radio in St Louis before she was hired at KATZ-AM 1600. She later moved to Detroit, Michigan to host a talk show at WJLB-FM.

I was really surprised by what I considered a betrayal by Lewis and Hutchinson so I accepted a job at KIRL-AM 1460 in St. Charles. KIRL presented gospel and religious programming. Bill White, the owner, had always been a close friend and supporter, and co-owner Johnny Roland, also a close friend and a former all-pro running back for the St.Louis Football Cardinals. I worked as a producer, salesman and air personality, but the station was a low power facility and the signal was directed to the rural areas of St. Charles County. I was successful on bringing in much needed sales for the station and I hosted a late night jazz show.

After a few months, in March of 1987 I left KIRL to become news director at KWMU-90.7 FM. KWMU, the 100,000 watts Public Radio station licensed to the University of Missouri-St. Louis. The facility was affiliated with National Public Radio (NPR) and American Public Radio (APR). I was the only African American in charge of a predominantly white newsroom in the Midwest. The format was classical music, news and jazz.

I was happy to be back in the Midwest and happy to be working in the medium that I loved. I did some reporting and anchoring at KWMU, and being a public radio station a lot of fund raising was included. Fund drives were four times a year and often there would be special promotions to raise additional revenue that required making personal appearances.

During this period I continued to monitor local commercial radio stations, did record hops and played music for special events, such as parties and reunions. I also kept apprised of FCC rules and regulations relating to the industry. I noticed that more and more of the local commercial stations were playing recordings with lewd and denigrating lyrics towards women, and continually using the N word. And it appeared that the same artists and recordings were played over and over again.

The announcers were young and evidently not well trained as announcers or deejays. It was obvious they knew nothing of the history or the struggle their predecessors endured nor did they seem to care. I also detected that most music videos were not at all diverse. The group of practitioners that produced and starred in these music productions used only nearly white or very light skinned dancers and other participants. This was certainly no strategy designed to reduce prejudice and promote tolerance. It only supported the theory some held that the lighter the skin, the better-quality the person. It certainly did not make or promote a more tolerant environment for individuals with darker skin tones. The roots of prejudice run deep and the producers of these videos only promoted intolerance and prejudice, even among African Americans.

New borderlines of taste were established that no one would have dreamed of a few years earlier. The First Amendment was used as a justification to express outrageous forms of phrasing and relating to an audience, often ignoring respect. Their creativity overshadowed their need for decency and moral management. Some of the recording displayed antisocial lyrics creating ethical dilemmas for media outlets and parents. Where do you draw the line? What is free speech, censorship or moral judgment? Some actions of the Federal Communications Commission were a disappointment to me and to thousands of others. In September 1992, the Federal telecommunications law allowed companies, for the first time, to own two AM and two FM stations in the same market. This was a significant change in the rules and the attitude of the commission. It would prove to be devastating to some smaller operations, while beneficial to large companies.

In the spring of 1993 I received a call from Dr. Donald Suggs, the new publisher of the St. Louis American Newspaper, and Eric Clark, the managing editor, about resuming the column that I had started earlier in the early 70's. I was to do general news and features that related to the African American community and to the St. Louis area, as well as national events that impacted the local area. The column was called "Bernie Hayes Understands", and it ran every Thursday in the weekly newspaper.

I concentrated mostly on controversial topics of interest to the local citizenry. Subjects such as local school board issues; racial and sex discrimination in the police and fire departments; employment biases; local and regional elections; local politics; housing discrimination and other issues that impacted mostly the African American community.

I gained national attention from the column. Because the paper was accessible from the World Wide Web, thousands of readers across the nation responded to my column and to the points of view that I expressed in the paper. Some were negative but most of the letters and telephone calls that I received were supportive and encouraging.

1993 was an eventful year. In March five people were arrested for the bombing of World Trade Center in New York and two police were officers convicted on federal civil rights charges in Rodney King beating, Ruth Bader Ginsburg was appointed to the U.S. Supreme Court, and Toni Morrison was awarded a Nobel Peace Prize for Literature.

The economic downturn threatened to reshape media landscape and it was felt in Public Radio as well as in the commercial medium. In March of 1993, I received a call from Roderick "Dr. Jockenstein" King, who was working at the local Noble Radio stations, Majic 108-FM and KATZ-AM 1600. I was asked to return to KATZ to do a morning talk show. Jacor, who was buying radio stations around the nations and becoming one of the nations largest broadcast businesses, finally took control of KATZ-AM, as I will illustrate in this chapter.

I met with the program director Chuck Atkins, and was offered a three-year contract. My shift was to be from 6am until 10am, Monday through Friday, with automatic quarterly raises with incentive bonuses. By agreeing to leave KWMU and to consent to work at KATZ, I would loose ten thousand dollars in yearly salary; six weeks of yearly vacation days and several days of yearly sick and personal leave time.

I thought over the proposition very carefully, but what I wanted most was to get information back to the people. Issues of racism and bias, affirmative action, and other complex and pressing problems were common in the community. I thought that by once again having a talk and information show, the people would benefit so I accepted the offer and I resigned from KWMU. I felt I should attempt to make a positive contribution to people who had suffered discrimination and injustices over the years.

My talk show was again a big hit in the area, with regular guests that included local mayors, and St. Louis County Executives, the Urban League, NAACP, school board presidents, entertainers and newsmakers as well as local civic and social organizations. I was an outlet for anyone and everyone who had an issue or a cause, and the flow of vital information was priceless. The main drawback was, the station did not provide me with a producer. I had to pay for my long distance telephone calls; personally contact and schedule my guests; answer the telephone and fulfill all of the duties a fulltime producer would perform. It was difficult and at times, frustrating.

Even with the distress and difficulty, I was pleased with the show. My guests, my listeners, the many groups and organizations that were a part of the program were quite happy with the show. The entire metropolitan region was buzzing with positive feedback. I had very good ratings and the program was completely sold out.

After six months, one of the local deejays with no experience in radio or the St. Louis market suggested to Chuck Atkins that I play more music with less talk in the morning, because the other stations were playing music. Although my ratings were higher than the music stations, Atkins told me what the deejay had proposed and suggested me drop most of my scheduled guests and change the program to a typically music format. I reminded Atkins that I left KWMU to come to KATZ to do a talk show, and I reminded him that was what we agreed on, but he was obstinate about the change, so the following Monday morning, I started the music format.

That morning, as soon as the switchboard was opened, the station was swarmed with protest calls, and soon after, pickets appeared at the station, demanding the talk show be reinstated. The community was outraged and they organized and demonstrated at the station and called for a boycott of the stations' sponsors until they restored my program as it had been.

I was eventually called in by station management and ordered to have the protesters stop their demon stations and to tell them that all was well. I refused and I was subsequently fired. The demonstrations continued and sponsors began to feel the damage of the boycott. Now the local press had become involved and the station was experiencing some really adverse publicity.

The public actions continued for more than a month so I was eventually contacted by the station and asked to mediate a settlement with the public. I again refused, as a result some local activists led by Percy Green, Norman Seay, Jamala Rogers, and Clifford Wilson, Sr.; Alderman Velma Jean Bailey, Alderman Irene J. Smith, Malik Ahmed, James Buford, Walle Amusa and others, met with the station's management and discussed ways to resolve the dispute. During this crisis, the owner of Noble Broadcasting came to St. Louis to meet with the group. Management denied that I had been fired. They called it a disagreement although I had not worked nor had I been paid for the time that I was off.

It was evident that the station was not pleased with the activists or with me. The talks generated resistance and conflict from the station and intense debate. After a few negotiating sessions the station agreed to restore the program and me, but the hours would be from 5 am until 9am, and yet without a producer or any help from the station. Upon my return only a few of the station employees would speak to me or communicate with me in any way. Only one of the more than twenty white workers would talk to me, and only a couple of the more than thirty African Americans would chat. They were afraid that if they became too chummy with me there would be repercussions to them.

Management had created and prolonged a conflict that should have been settled. I was in a very unique position but I decided to restore my reputation as a community person and offered various groups and organizations another vehicle for empowerment. Soon afterward, Noble Broadcast Group sold out to Jacor Broadcasting, and thereby becoming the nation's fifth's largest radio company at that time.

During this period, the FCC was steadily deregulating the broadcast industry. The commission removed most restrictions on ownership, allowing broadcast mergers, and giving more power to the powerful. Over a period of a few months more than 1,000 corporate mergers were planned in broadcasting and nearly half of the country's radio stations changed hands. Today, according to the government's figures, the top three broadcasters control at least 60 percent of the stations in the top 100 markets in the country.

From their Internet Homepage Clear Channel submits "Clear Channel Worldwide (Clear Channel Communications, Inc., NYSE: CCU), headquartered in San Antonio, TX, is a global leader in the out-of-home advertising industry with radio and television stations, outdoor displays, and entertainment venues in 66 countries around the world. Including announced transactions, Clear Channel operates approximately 1,225 radio and 39 television stations in the United States and has equity interests in over 240 radio stations internationally. Clear Channel also operates approximately 776,000 outdoor advertising displays, including billboards, street furniture and transit panels around the world. Clear Channel Entertainment is a leading promoter, producer and marketer of live entertainment events and also owns leading athlete management and marketing companies".

With conglomerates such as Clear Channel, a small, independent radio station or record label could hardly compete. The company's music practices have been challenged by several national and regional independent record labels, and by consumer advocate Ralph Nader. Nader criticized the broadcast industry's new consolidation rules declared that the FCC should investigate payments to radio stations for airplay. He compared the policy to the payola scandals and practices of the 1960s.

Another of the corporate communications giants is Emmis Communications. Emmis Communications owns and operates radio, television and magazine entities in large and medium sized markets throughout the U.S., and is the 7th largest radio group in the U.S.

And there is Radio One, Inc., owned by African American Cathy Hughes, and managed by her son Alfred Liggins. It is the largest African American owned and operated broadcast-company in the nation. It has stations in several major markets, and it is now a public company. The company is worth more than $2 billion dollars. Her stations now reach over 18 million Black listeners daily.

Hughes and her company has been described as "the voice of the Black community", noted for its talk and information formats, but with her St. Louis station, WFUN 95.5 FM, the format is Rap and hip-hop, with many of the songs containing lyrics some consider lewd and indecent. The St. Louis market always appears to get programming of poorer quality. The St. Louis facility appeared to ignore the needs of the public it serves, virtually ignoring events that impact the daily lives of its listeners.

Hughes has been applauded for increasing opportunities for minorities and women and for its intense community involvement, except in the St. Louis market. Again, the format and programming is directed to the 18-24 year old, competing with Clear Channels KMJM and 103.3 FM. It is a scenario once again of the greed that drives the corporate leaders. Hughes dedication to minority communities seemed to be missing in the St. Louis market.

CHAPTER 19

The Poor Gets Poorer!

A provocative premise is that some African Americans are as much to blame for the decline in Black ownership as the rules implemented by the Federal Communications Commission. The conglomerates are certainly in control of the airwaves, and the number of independent stations is dropping, because of the 1996 Telecommunications Act that allowed the big companies to acquire as many stations as possible by abandoning the nationwide ownership limit as we earlier described. Voices in the African American communities were slowly diminishing and the phrase 'diversity' was not a consideration. The result also was fewer blacks are employed within the industry. The impact was damaging and destructive. The National Association of Black Owned Broadcasters (NABOB) fought deregulation but the FCC essentially ignored their demands. Proponents of deregulation convinced the FCC that radio broadcasters needed to grow in order to compete with other large media companies.

There are some black-owned broadcasters attempting to buy more stations but the capital is not easy to obtain. Stations in the Carolinas, and other southern cities fought hard to buy facilities that were already broadcasting, or negotiating to get new frequencies. Minority tax certificates were eliminated and with fewer radio stations available, the possibility of increasing the number of minority owned facilities is more or less impossible.

Although federal law prohibits radio stations from taking money or anything of value in exchange for playing songs without disclosing the payment to listeners, the major radio stations are easily avoiding the rule.

Discrimination also is playing a significant role in minority ownership. Minorities, including Blacks, Hispanics, Asians, and Native Americans together represent nearly 1/3 of the U.S. population; they have never owned more than 3 % of the nation's broadcast stations. Minority ownership of TV stations is also steadily declining. This is further proof that the decrease in minority ownership is because of deregulation in the media industry, thus resulting in economic pressures in broadcasting that force many operators out of business.

Very few broadcasters appeared to be interested in developing new innovative programs designed to offer the public challenging and professional music or information programs. It appeared the landscape was void of leadership that offered education, specialized skills, and diversified experiences in the media directed to the African American community. I thought the industry should present leadership by providing opportunities for professional development and create innovative ideas and programs, and train a new generation of musical and cultural leaders.

In today's business world, with its ever-changing marketplace, I felt it would come into view that many or most of the music and broadcasting companies would recognize the need to adapt and change in order to fulfill a commitment to their listeners; thereby remaining competitive by serving the community and subsequently increasing profits. The persons who were in charge were unable to identify opportunities for change. They identified their listener's needs but failed to implement strategies to supply their requirements. In this situation, the executives failed to gather solid input while disrespecting and paying no heed to the people.

We all recognize the need for increased minority growth and ownership of media outlets in order to ensure that all Americans are represented and their voices are heard. But with the creation of media mergers and buyouts of minority-owned broadcast stations, the plight of minority media is more disappointing now than ever. The lack of available resources has led several minority-owned media companies to sell to or merge with mainstream media companies, and the outlook is bleak. Minority ownership is at an all time low, down 14% since 1997. Only 4% of radio stations and 1.9% of television stations are minority owned.

Diversity became a non-issue with the more lenient ownership rules, especially under the Reagan and both Bush administrations. The number of individual radio station owners declined by one fourth. It substantiates the argument that minorities have lost opportunities because of media consolidations. These actions naturally result in the decline in different voices and viewpoints, and decrease employment opportunities for minorities in broadcasting. The gap between the rich and the poor keeps growing, keeping the underdog virtually in poverty without much hope for future ownership or inclusion. For the poor and minorities the practices of the FCC in coercion with the media giants this creates another set of critical issues and dilemmas. There is no hint of corporate consciousness among some of the people who run the agency and their cohort owners., Black owners are as to blame as white corporations in the demise of Black radio.

Some African American and Hispanics have attempted to remain in business and penetrate the communications industry by considering to purchase low-power TV stations, or to provide programming to established full-power stations, as a method of gaining ownership, although the number of minority television station owners also decreased substantially. There are groups that provide internships to minority students in television and radio. The National Association of Black Journalists and Media Careers for Minorities are two such organizations. The National Association of Black Journalists (NABJ) 'is an organization of journalists, students and media-related professionals that provides quality programs and services to and advocates on behalf of black journalists worldwide'. It was established in1975, in Washington, D.C. to serve black journalists nationwide, and they have don an excellent job. I became a member in the St. Louis chapter in 1980.

CHAPTER 20

Black Radio is abandoned!

The days of personality radio were big because the local disc jockeys were devotedly aware of their listener's interest in community news and weather forecasts, and they became highly competitive in seeking to appeal to a new audience. For many years the local personalities provided comprehensive coverage of issues and information with extensive emphasis being given to particular areas. These shows contained the music, the entertainment, and the reports that let the listeners know they were cared about. The announcers usually shared the same problems and the same tribulations as their listeners, and situations in urban communities were the same all over the nation. The morning personalities in most urban and rural areas kept the community informed with comprehensive details of the deeds, actions and events around town. The rural dwellers got farm reports and information from the local farm bureaus, and what little they could extract from some University Extension programs.

In both urban and rural settings, the 'jocks' spoke the language or dialect that connected them to their audiences and admirers, while delivering important messages that gave the listeners a sense of personal communication. Most had dedication or talkback telephone lines in their studios, particularly the well-known radio personalities. The impact of this 'personalization' was brilliant and valuable, for it gave both parties a sense of intimacy and feedback. In many instances, the announcers had the ability to shape human life. They were entertainers and salespersons. The jocks were reaching communities that others had forgotten or disregarded. They reached people who live in areas with no phones and no electricity. They reached people who could not read or write. Even in the poorest rural and urban communities, the people listened. People were encouraged to help themselves, and where to get help. Radio was the medium of choice, and at times it was the only medium.

Black people would trust the news they received from their jocks, because they knew there was a big difference between the so-called 'mainstream and tabloid coverage' and the information they received from the persons they knew and trusted. Some of the criticisms cited lack of objectivity, factual inaccuracies, sensationalism and negativism in the Black community. Since either local owners or corporate ownership dictates the flow of news and information, most Black people depended on the radio and Black newspapers to get the information they needed and wanted.

Most radio and television stations rely on focus groups and professional demographers for information they need to be directed at their specific audiences. Some target the younger set because of the changing racial and ethnic composition of the kids' population. Factors include the buyers' activities in the kids market, trends and an analysis of the buying method of families with kids.

Teens are the target of most radio stations targeting the African American community. The teen market includes more than 35 million young American consumers ages 10 to 18. The companies know where they live, how many work, and how much their household earns They k now their buying habits and how much time they spend on the Internet. They know what brands are favorites and their shopping and buying habits. Perhaps one of the most important factors is the music they buy and listen to. This is why record companies represent a huge part of the music industry, and how they affect the formats of radio stations.

Record companies have formed an alliance with radio stations to get their product played on the air, and the radio stations wants to be first to play new material for their listeners. It is a win-win situation for both because record companies make their money by selling compacts discs, and radio stations make money by selling airtime to advertisers. These are the driving forces of the industry, and although African Americans spend billions of dollars on the products that are advertised on radio and television, seldom do radio stations consider their community requirements or requests. The majority of the time that the station speaks directly to the African American consumer is for entertainment promotions and performances.

By accenting key characteristics of the teen population, such as race and ethnicity, projected population growth, and employment and income patterns, and teen-buying power, station professionals study trends in the teen market such as their impact on family buying decisions. By ignoring the wishes and wants of the African American population, the stations program a steady diet of non-meaningful music that keeps the audience ignorant of important civic, political and social issues, while the radio station is undisturbed and grossing enormous profits.

Our ethnic makeup, economic status and our educational achievements are fundamental changes that have come in recent years. The Baby Boom demographic phenomenon is probably the most significant factor that impacts radio programs directed to Blacks. The stations came up with the 'old school' or 'oldie' format to appease and placate older listeners. Nothing like the personality jocks of earlier years, when you would hear the music you grew to love and enjoy. In fact, the new breed of announcers for the most part, has no familiarity with the communications industry. Some are hired because of their 'hip' speech and fly dress. Some are college trained but still cannot connect with their past or associate or identify with anyone over thirty years old.

Also, the crumbling of family values and the rise in single parent families has, unfortunately, been a major factor in categorizing Black people as poor, and unworthy of concern. The 'Blaxploitation' movies made a lot of Black people believe hat what they saw on the screen really represented them, and some lost any inspiring thoughts or goals. The genre also led to the destruction of moral and social values in today's 'hip-hop' lyrical structures.

Older persons of African decent are in a special category in America. The labor shortages and skills gaps that have persisted in the late 1990's continue today, and the future of this country actually lies in large part with its minority populations. The populations that are ignored by radio stations and other media outlets. The current folds of jocks, both male and female, Black and white, do not have a clue on how this negatively impacts the population at large. They should be promoting family values with their music, instead of denigrating women. They should be promoting positive manhood and womanhood.

It is a known fact that children who are regularly and positively connected to their fathers tend to do better in school, avoid involvement with the juvenile justice system, and have more positive relationships with their peers. Fathers want to contribute to the well being of their children, and the music they hear should reinforce these positions and encourage fathers to be responsible.

These and several other elements contributed to the **'death of black radio'.** Most program directors of today's urban stations will not play an R&B recording. Although the advertise themselves as 'Hip-Hop and R&B', these Negro wannabe Whites will be the first to tell you that 'this record is ***too urban*** or ***does not have enough crossover appeal*'** for our audience. They have become the tools of their masters as some of their Negro predecessors have been.

Urban and rural youth are vulnerable to these problems. It is my belief that Hip-Hop and rap recordings that promote the gangster lifestyle are detrimental to young minds. I understand most youth will argue that they can make the distinction between recordings and reality, but do the statistics support this contention? Drug and alcohol abuse, gang activity, adolescent pregnancy, and homelessness are just a few of the problems confronting today's urban children. I understand that only a small percentage of kids are negatively influenced, but I believe one is too many. All of them should be exposed to radio broadcasts that encourage positive youth development alternatives rather than hard-core activity.

The graphic depiction of women as sexual objects and victims of brutality and violence certainly impacts society as a whole. It affects social structure and in my judgment, promotes social dysfunction.

I personally believe that the portrayal of violence in music videos and in the lyrics of some rap recordings encourages violent behavior. The relationship between media and crime is vague. I do believe that there is a psychological, political, social and in some cases, a developmental consequence from the portrayals in these videos and in 'gangsta rap' lyrics.

Some record companies have placed parental advisory labels on their recorded material, and the Recording Industry of America voluntarily labels CDs it deems inappropriate for children. I am sure we all agree that free speech is a cherished right, but under FCC rules and federal law, radio stations and over-the-air television channels cannot air material that refers to sexual and excretory functions between 6 a.m. and 10 p.m., when children may be tuning in.

Religious leaders, and religious organizations, community activists, as well as individual citizens, should criticize and act in response when vulgar and obscene songs are broadcast. Criticism of the media by telephone is not an effective method to get the stations to stop playing such songs. The most assured course would be to demonstrate at the station, or attempt to convince the facilities sponsors that they should withhold their advertising from the station until the music became less objectionable. Everyone in the community should be concerned, and the negativity associated with media outlets should be enough to persuade the owners and programmers to present line-ups and shows that stress positive images.

In the meantime, there are some black oriented stations in the South and a few smaller urban station north of the Mason-Dixon line that still have the 'personality' type jock that mimic or carry out the format of old-time black radio. Some know the history of black personality radio', while others do not and there are some who are not concerned.

Al Benson is a great example of the personality that African Americans in broadcasting exemplified in the 'good old days' of radio. Although I outlined Benson in earlier chapters, he was talked about in both positive and negative terms while he ruled the airways in Chicago in the 40's, 50's, until the early 60's. He spoke with a black Southern accent and used neighborhood slang on the air. He played black hits and established the Rhythm and Blues format. Even some of the newer jocks in these small urban and rural communities, especially in the inner city, are considered celebrities but some are courting white teens as opposed to their rhythm and blues followers. The station management and owners want to charm white general market ratings, and yet call themselves a 'black' station. African American listeners and consumers are the losers.

Unlike conventional radio stations, black oriented stations are usually the poorest, because an advertiser fails to recognize the station's potential and virtually ignores the millions of dollars in this consumer group. Hardly ever do radio outlets directed to African Americans reflect and build on ideas of great things that black people have achieved in the world, and for the world. Except for a few Black talk shows, these accomplishments are shared only in Black History Month..

When it comes to meaningful programming, Black people are as deprived today as they were in the early days of radio. They were not then, and very rarely now are we exposed to groundbreaking and pioneering historical events made by Africans or African Americans. Favors are the driving engines that usually determine what is broadcast to us. Corporate ownership of the press and most media outlets constrict the flow of ideas, and also unfairly deprive smaller radio stations and recordings artists' from receiving equal treatment. When it comes to fairness and impartiality, the business has reverted back to the days when payola was rampant. It is a true statement that who owns the media is in control.

As a common practice, some record companies are partnering with certain radio stations that appear to be payola, or play- for- play. Record companies 'buying' promotion time for guaranteed airplay for particular songs or albums are deals that appear to be shady. Independent promoters, working for record companies, make payments to music directors or other radio station executives, to promote new songs. These practices manipulate retail sales and seem to ignore business and moral ethics. We become the victims of these customs and corrupt traditions because countless people buy records exclusively on what they hear on the radio.

Radio stations also request record companies to send in acts free for a station promotion, or a concert. This helps the radio station boost their ratings, thereby increasing revenue; and the record company will most likely receive a guarantee that the artists and others on the particular label will have their product played on that station. This sometimes backfires also, because with such fierce competition among radio stations in certain markets, if a band comes in for one station, another station might take the labels current records off the air. It is a common practice in the industry.

Because of record companies and radio stations working in concert and in effect dominating the industry, many artists began creating their own independent labels, and taking their chances in the marketplace. Some are very good business professional, while for the most part, the smaller and less edu-cated performers find themselves at the mercy of unscrupulous promoters or distributors. They usually cannot demand the radio play needed to properly promote their product, but they do have control.

A few major companies control the majority the music industry: Sony Music Entertainment; Universal Music Group; BMG Entertainment and EMI: these are the parent companies or distributors of Arista, RCA, A&M, Decca, Rhino, Deutsche Grammophon, Odeon, Parlophone, Island, MCA, Motown, Polydor, Columbia, Epic, Angel, Blue Note, Capitol, Virgin, Atlantic, Elektra, London, Reprise, and many others. These companies control 75-85% of global music production.

CHAPTER 21

Black has always been beautiful!

Despite what history books teach about the hardships of African Americans on these shores, there are thousands of encouraging stories to tell. Encouraging and positive historical information should be a daily part of each broadcast day on stations programming to the African American community.

A countless number of people of African decent operated successful businesses in the majority society. Many opened and ran companies between 1910 and 1940. Even though our ancestors were forbidden to attend schools, and were not allowed to learn to read or write, many challenged the establishment, and acquired the skills needed to run small businesses and farms. They learned economic strategies and learned the capitalist system. There were several Black businesses in San Francisco, Los Angeles and Oakland in the nineteenth century, and Black entrepreneurs, regardless of the racism and bias they faced, found themselves prospering as barbers, boot blacks, livery stable owners and attendants, while some owned restaurants and laundries. These facts should be told.

Most African Americans know about the prosperous, all-black community in North Tulsa, Oklahoma in the early 1900's that was once generally referred to as "Black Wall Street" or "Little Africa", but it is seldom written or talked about. There were black-owned retail stores, restaurants, doctors and nurses, financial institutions, and law offices. Also during the 1920's, a thriving black business district was located in Charlottesville, Virginia. Referred to as Vinegar Hill, Main Street had restaurants, grocers, barbershops, poolrooms, furniture stores, fish markets, drug stores, professional offices, and cleaners.

Very little is known about our past in St. Augustine, Florida. America's oldest city has the distinction of as being the site of the first free black community in the United States in the 18th century, and the southernmost beginning point of the Underground Railroad.

Black people also help settle the West. Even in areas near where York, whom I consider the real leader, led the Lewis and Clark expedition, by showing Lewis and Clark how to survive, more than 200 years ago. In the early 1900's in Tucson,

Arizona, many early African American settlers owned car repair shops and service stations, restaurants, shoeshine parlors and many other small businesses.

Closer to home, in Memphis' between 1860 and 1870, African-Americans, celebrating their new found freedom, owned hundreds of businesses. They were leaders in social, political and economic activities. A three-day riot in 1866 wiped out most of the gains black people had worked and labored for.

St. Louis, Missouri has a rich African American history also. Blacks accompanied Pierre Laclede in 1764 to the trading post that is now the City of St. Louis. Hardly anyone ever tells the story of a mulatto woman named Ester, who owned land on what is now Laclede's Landing on the St. Louis Riverfront. It is a little known fact that Blacks were killed defending St. Louis from the British in the Revolutionary War. The historic Dred Scott freedom trial was held in 1847 at the Old Courthouse in downtown St. Louis. There is so much to tell. I am sure there are stories and accounts of Blacks making significant contributions wherever they settled in this country.

And Chicago had an area called 'Black Metropolis', and 'Bronzeville', the area that I was raised. These areas were significantly urbanized in the 1920s through the 1940s. African Americans have been in the Chicago area since 1834. Most put down roots in the area known as North Shore, near Evanston. As described in previous chapters, the need for workers in the city's factories and stockyards led to thousands of African-Americans from the deep south settling in Chicago as part of "The Great Migration". The city was called "The Promised Land". On both the South Side and the West Side, Blacks created major business districts, churches, theaters and cultural institutions.

Every Black radio station in the country should promote the struggles and accomplishments of past and current offerings of our ancestors that have contributed to the growth of America. People should be told and who better than their own to tell it? Radio stations are portable and powerful modes of communicating, and can have an effect on politicians, businesspersons, educators, and entertainers. The influence can either be positive or negative. The programming can be decent and high quality or shocking and appalling.

I want to again be reminiscent that in the early days, African American announcers challenged bigotry, racism, stereotypes, Jim Crow segregation, low, and sometimes *no* wages, and other hardships to pave the way for the voices and faces that are on the air today. They survived the depression, World War II, and the impact of intolerance and prejudice. The early pioneers and innovators established a culture and wholesome traditions that changes social and economic conditions, and influenced their listener's interactions with others. . They spread the word and established and rooted religious and secular music. These pioneers also played a vital part in establishing cultural norms and a national agenda to gain equality and parity.

CHAPTER 22

Black Radio Music Stations seem opposed to News and Talk!

In 1979 the economy and the lack of advertising revenue had triggered a number of layoffs in the industry, and for stations targeting the African American market, the news departments were the first to feel the crunch. As a consequence, the quality of news production suffered. Early in the year Jack Gibson, aka 'Jockey Jack' and 'Jack The Rapper' called me while I was on the air on KATZ—AM and told me that he was elated but surprised that I had begun a talk show on a station that had been a pioneering force in Black radio. He also believed that talk radio would be the salvation of failing black A M stations.

AM is short for _amplitude modulation_, a method used to modulate and transmit radio signals, compared to _frequency modulation_ or FM, which is can transmit in either analog or digital form. FM requires a wider bandwidth but make the signal more powerful. Since most of the country had become accustomed to FM programming, talk and information or religious programming appeared the best way for the small, independent A M stations to survive.

In fact the first black radio announcers' hosted news and talk shows combined with some music, normally gospel or religious. As early as 1935, in southern and northern cities, several white owned stations around the country presented 15 to 30 minute programs featuring Black announcers giving news and information to the African American community.

W. Leonard Evans established the National Negro Network, on January 20, 1954. It was the fist African American-owned radio network and it transmitted to 40 stations. It was timely also because only a few months later, the network provided inside information on Brown V. Board of Education, the landmark suit that ended racial discrimination in public schools, and the appointment of Ralph J. Bunche, the first black winner of the Nobel Peace Prize, as undersecretary to the United Nations. Because of the Brown V. Board decision, schools in Washington, D.C. and Baltimore, Maryland were also desegregated. Black stations recognized the need for news departments also during the Montgomery, Alabama bus boycott, and the Emmet Til murder and trial in Mississippi. The action of civil rights marchers and organizations made it a must for news of the movement to reach the African American community and to the general public.

These were important stories to African Americans, who had been considered not worthy of information, because they had virtually been overlooked and disregarded in all areas. Issues of race, economics, politics, safety, medical, legal, professional and other significant topics, and important news stories were usually not broadcast to black listeners.

In 1956, I began delivering community and national news in my disc jockey show at KDBS in Alexandria, Louisiana, and the impact was so great, and the news was so received that black businesses came to the station to purchase airtime to be delivered during the newscasts. The community was interested and curious about civil rights activities and news in general. The white owners were more than surprised to see the reaction of the community to my news reports. I was called from as far away as New Orleans to give information on certain reports.

In later years, the power and value of news broadcasts to the African American community became evident to radio station owners and programmers. In 1964, Roy Wood propelled WVON in Chicago to number one in the city, principally because of the news department, of which I was a member. Wesley South's Hotline commenced in 1962 and it was the most listened to discussion and information radio show in the city as I have previously described. The community responded encouragingly to the news and information it received and the ratings and sales reflected as much. Accurate and objective information began to flow to the diverse communities all over the region and conditions were improved for the masses. Leonard Chess, the owner of WVON also instituted a major news department at WNOV, its station in Milwaukee. Soon after, other Black oriented stations followed the Chess formula and began integrating a major presence in their daily broadcast day. That station today has an all news and talk format.

In 1972, The Mutual Broadcasting Network launched the Mutual Black Network. It was later changed to the Sheridan Network, but many Black oriented stations subscribed to the service, and the news was first class, delivered by professionals, but the feeds were not of the best quality to some of their stations.

Later the National Black Network was introduced and the feature was almost an instant winner. All of these organizations were comparable to any of the major network's operations.

Bob Law

The media equations would never be equal simply because of the disparity in net worth. News had changed the role of communications in Black society. It affected our social structure and got people connected to the political structure. Public opinions were being changed and public debates were instigated and put into action. The character and influence of these news programs and some of their innovations were seen in cultural changes and transformation in communications. The Black networks and news services had millions of listeners in many major U.S. cities. The oral historians had finally arrived.

One of the most popular and informative news and informational programs was "Night Talk", hosted by Bob Law and originating from WWRL-AM in Queens, New York. It was a national show with call in participation and regular guests from around the nation. It was broadcast locally in St. Louis on KATZ-AM, the same facility that my talk show was aired.

Bob and I became the very best of friends and he made frequent speaking and social visits to St. Louis and other cities in the vicinity. He proved that talk shows were popular and needed.

Despite the mass move toward privatization, talk shows, especially in the African American community is needed to explore so many issues and develop strategies to overcome the many problems facing the Black community. The relationship between media and politics is most important and talk shows the vehicles needed to examine topics and focus on matters of concern. In the Black community, there is a need for more competition in broadcasting.

Some Black Talk Shows are meant to mislead and mis-educate!

The dynamics of electronic politics and mainstream talk demonstrates how color and race combine to challenge the common presumption that the press is strongly liberal. Examining the controversy these subjects often evoke, talk shows offers a glimpse at both ethical and historical factors on both sides of the issues. Addressing the value of public opinion, talk shows examine how the nation is dealing with these stories.

Conservative talk show hosts Larry Elder and Allan Keyes, although both are very articulate, I believe they are misleading their audiences and are operatives of the persons who are making an effort to keep Black people dependent on the government and at the mercy of big business. To me, they are the Clarence Thomas' of media. They are the best things that could happen for the conglomerates. I think they spread propaganda for corporate and personal gain. In my opinion they are against the interests of the people who are seeking self-determination and free will either enthusiastically or reluctantly, the results are the same.

Larry Elder is a talk show host on KABC Talk Radio in Los Angeles. His nationally syndicated show is on daily from 3 p.m. to 7 p.m. He is known as the "Sage From South Central,"

Alan Keyes is very controversial among Black people and white people. He has been accused by some of running for the Presidential nomination to raise his profile and help his career as a public speaker and radio personality.

Both seem to have organized movements against poor people and people of color and joined the ultra-conservatives that preach unity while distorting facts and stories important to the survival of ordinary people. I associate them with Russ Limbaugh. I believe they all exist to promote the most offensive ideas and controversial issues strictly for personal gains. In my opinion, Rush Limbaugh was one of the worst things that could have happened to talk radio. I think he was thrust upon us as some form of punishment.

Rush espouses conservative ideology while distorting facts, and that is scary because he is a heard daily on over 600 radio stations, reaching over 20 million listeners a week.

Because a few black-formatted stations are successful in some of the largest U.S. cities, most black owned station are struggling. The flourishing stations have almost abandoned what was called a Black format and developed or adopted a mostly mainstream and commercial design, preferring to not to address critical news and civic issues, and playing what they consider the hits and targeting young audiences.

Deregulation and mergers has all but destroyed urban radio, and in some cases, the urban community. Downsizing and format changes have removed black employment and black empowerment. We now have the least number of black-owned stations in many years, and the trend of bankers and financiers is to fund the 'haves' and not the 'have nots'. In other words, the money is going to the multiple ownership deals as opposed to persons wanting to buy or expand. Proving again that the big gets bigger and the small just get lost. The opportunities are fewer and the future looks bleak.

There is hope all the same. I believe the future lie in a new, diverse generation of African American broadcasters who are Afrocentric, and are interested in exploring key issues in media, and who are ethical, intellectual and somewhat experts in social responsibility.

Cornel West, a Professor of Religion and African American Studies at Princeton University, is one of the new class of award winning journalists who are on the front line of the business of monitoring public behavior. West is the voice of conscious for hundreds of thousands.

One of the leading talk show hosts and commentators is **Tavis Smiley**. He once hosted the BET Network late-night TV talk show and is currently heard on National Public Radio and seen on the Tavis Smiley Show on PBS. Smiley is often called 'the voice of Black America', and is an author of several books.

And there is Tom Joyner, from our KWK days, which became the first African American to be elected to the Radio Hall of Fame. Tom Joyner was nicknamed "The Fly Jock" and "The Hardest Working Man in Radio" by working long hours and flying between his morning job (in Dallas, Texas) and afternoon job (in Chicago, Illinois) every weekday for years. He and I worked together at KWK in St.Louis. The ABC radio network syndicates the Tom Joyner Morning Show.

The social responsibility with regard to Black radio listeners by Black owners is frequently nonexistent. Corporate social responsibility is usually measured by the margin of profit of the owners. The higher the profit, the more consideration management considers approaching delicate issues, but usually the persons in charge do not mind alienating employees or their listeners when their earnings are at stake.

A good example is the recent program changes at The Inner City Broadcasting Corporation (ICBC) that operates New York's radio station WLIB-1190 AM. In March 2004, it was revealed that WLIB-1190 A M, a station that had has been devotedly working in and for New York's Black community would be forming an alliance with the predominately White, liberal talk-radio network Air America Radio. In the early '90s WLIB was praised and recognized as a resource for "Afrocentric" programming, but Inner City's chairman, Pierre Sutton, an African American and the son of Percy Sutton, explained that their method of attracting new listeners would be by using "progressive activists" and "celebrities". He asserted that those efforts 'countered the national popularity of White, Right-wing conservative talk shows and radio personalities'.

The move by Sutton and his new partners put more Black professionals out work, and substantially hampered the free flow of information to the African American community. When WLIB joined with Air America Radio, only a few of the leading Black radio personalities on the station kept their jobs.

Another devastating blow to talk show fans was the decision of NPR to replace 30-year NPR veteran broadcaster and host of *Morning Edition* Bob Edwards. His last program was aired April 30, 2004, and the radio waves lost another award-winning advocate of fairness and human rights. *Morning Edition* is the 2nd most listened-to national radio program in the country.

Edwards joined NPR in 1974 when the organization was in its third year. He was a newscaster and later co-host of All Things Considered before moving to Morning Edition as its original host in November 1979.

CHAPTER 23

Raunchy Urban Music predates Hip-Hop!

Although a considerable quantity of the lyrics of popular Hip-hop and rap music seem appalling and shocking to some, the style is not new to the African American community, or to the music industry. I do not know if the portrayal of violence in the media or on recordings encourages violent acts, or whether brutal actions encourage artists to write the music. I believe there is no place for violence in music entertainment. Why should women be depicted as sexual objects and victims of violence? Promoting violence against women or other members of society is absurd, yet dehumanizing lyrics, suggestive words and lewd and indecent metaphors are common themes in the radio, television, video and movie industry, and it is all profit motivated.

Sex has always been a topic that has pushed the boundaries of decency in the recording industry. Some of the best-known and loved African American personalities have occasionally recorded songs that have been considered vulgar or too suggestive and were barred from the airways. Tongue-in-cheek humor was considered naughty but harmless to some, depending on the degree of bawdiness; and to others nothing short of censorship would be sufficient.

In 1920, Mamie Smith's 'Crazy Blues' was considered coarse. It was a national hit, played mostly on jukeboxes but did get some radio play. It sold over a million copies. During the 20's the jukebox was a black musicians main source of exposure. Radio stations would not play 'race records' and the music industry was as segregated as the nation. Most whites considered black music 'unacceptable'.

However some of the most popular white authors in the early years were accused of producing indecent material. Cole Porter's recordings of "Let's Do It" and "Love for Sale," were banned from the air and Rodgers and Hammerstein's had to change the words to their song "My Boy Bill" in the musical Carousel, but the African American artists suffered more than any of the white composers or artists.

Radio station KWK—A M in St.Louis, Missouri, a station that I have fond memories of, and one of the stations I profiled in a previous chapter, was a leader in a censorship movement. KWK at different times was one of St.Louis' most popular radio stations in both the black and white communities. In 1958 the management of KWK called Rock n Roll 'undesirable music' and banned all of the music from the stations play list. Rock and Roll and the entire so-called Race music genre was under attack. White stations were not playing black music at this time anyhow

One of the first crossover artists, Chuck Berry was at first banned because he was black. KWK's action was in part brought because white kids liked Berry's music. At the time, St. Louis did not want the races mixed and Rock and Roll was contributing to this integration. Local white citizens were outraged because their children were fans of this black musician and singer.

Berry eventually became a favorite of both races but his recording 'My Ding-A-Ling' was viewed as unsuitable for airplay on some stations while it became a top ten hit on others. You can see the inconsistency because these situations illuminate the challenges for program directors and station managers.

How can Black artists cope in a society that promotes race instability and status differences? Race inequality in earnings, accommodations and airplay are the norm for most musicians of color.

Several black artists recordings were disapproved of, and in some instances banned from radio because of their lyrical content. One of the most popular singers and bandleaders of the early 40's and 50's was Bull Moose Jackson. Benjamin 'Bull Moose' Jackson began as a musician and singer in Lucky Millinder's band who later formed his own combo, 'The Buffalo Bearcats'. His recordings of 'Big Ten Inch Record', 'Nosey Joe' and 'Bow Legged Woman' were considered suggestive but became big hits for Jackson.

Roosevelt Sykes had several recordings that were considered smutty but he became a favorite of blues lovers all over the world. He also often toured and recorded with singer St. Louis Jimmy Oden, the originator of the classic "Going Down Slow."

Dinah Washington's 'Big Long Slidin' Thing' and 'Long John Blues' was considered bawdy with references to sex. The Dominoes 'Sixty Minute Man' had several naughty phrases and word of mouth propelled it to more than a million sales.

Hank Ballard and the Midnighters, who were previously 'The Royals', had a number of recordings that were prohibited from airplay but sold hundreds of thousands of records. "Work With Me Annie', 'Annie Had a Baby', 'Sex Ways', 'Annie's Aunt Fannie' and 'There's a Thrill Up on The Hill' were all best sellers from juke boxes, with very little radio exposure. "Mountain Oysters" by Eddie

"Lockjaw" Davis was another recording that was the subject of censorship; Wynonie Harris's hit in this genre was "*Wasn't That Good?*" Harris was considered the real King of Rock, before Elvis. His "Good Rockin' Tonight' was a remarkable success.

1964 The Kingsmen's version of "Louie, Louie" was considered 'dirty' simply because some people did not understand the words to the song. Since the monitors could not decipher the lyrics they thought the words were obscene.

As long as there have been recordings there have been those who have sought to control the content of such recordings. There are those who believe that we should think as they think and like what they like. They are usually the ones who try to restrict or control what we say, write, sing, record or broadcast. Almost everything is objectionable to one person or another, and certain persons want to supervise and control the recording and broadcast industries.

Censorship in music is a topic that has brought about much controversy. I do not advocate the censoring of compositions, but material that may be considered immoral, obscene or offensive should be concealed from children and kept in particular places with strong privacy safeguards. Our children, and young men and women are continually exposed to sexist, racist or otherwise vulgar lyrics and these recordings should be restricted from playing in a public place.

There is a current assortment of artists who are creating an intensity of obscene, vulgar, lewd, filthy and suggestive music. They have joined some of the older established performers who are known for music that contains sexual content and profane language. Leon Heywood was one of the first in the modern era to release a suggestive recording that became a top seller. His "I Want to Do Something Freaky to You' became a smash in the early 70's.

Millie Jackson had a string of hits with vulgar words and obscene suggestions, but most were played on the radio. She was in demand for personal appearances and her career flourished because of these recordings. Millie has been called the "Queen of Extreme".

Another woman who continue to push the boundaries of what some consider tolerable is Denise LaSalle. Denise is a master of self-expression and her recordings explores the limits of what could be considered morally depressing or improper.

Ruby Andrews who scored big with hits like "Casanova" and "You Made a Believer out of me" recorded a tune called 'Footprints on the ceiling' that raised quite a few eyebrows. Ruby contends these records are a matter of economic survival and provocative songs are accepted among her fans. If they produced an erotic idea, it was what the audience wanted and enjoyed.

Barbara Carr recorded several tunes that had sexual undertones and evocative lyrics. Her "Bone Me Like You Own Me" and several more of her tunes pleased her followers but some were in shock over the words and charges of immorality.

Marvin Sease recorded an album titled "Candy Licker' that clicked right away with most urban stations. It made him an instant star and he recorded several more in the same vein that did just as well. His 'Hoochie Mama' remained on the charts for months.

The 2004 recoding by Theodis Ealey entitled 'Stand Up In It 'also was considered smutty and indecent, but some urban radio stations programmed the recording without incident or complaints from the general public. Some of these recordings promote male chauvinism and sexism in addition to gender inequality.

Conclusion!

I hope the content of the book traced sufficiently the long history and struggle of the African American radio announcer and certain Blacks in the entertainment industry. I also hope that my story helps readers understand how I and others in the industry dealt with race, culture, gender, discrimination and bigotry and how we found ways to focus on positive development to defeat a disapproving structure.

From the first Africans brought to these shores as slaves, until today, Blacks have been communication specialists. First with drums and right up through the Harlem Renaissance, The Great Depression, World Wars and the Civil Rights movement, interaction has occurred and a new generation of raconteurs emerged.

I hope this book chronicles individual and shared Black achievement in the world's first mass broadcast medium. We have transitioned and transformed from being portrayed as clowns and buffoons to some of the nations and the worlds most influential writers, directors, producers, public relations specialists and announcers.

I also hope the current group of hip-hop and urban announcers adhere to the strict ethical standards the pioneers set.

I want to express my gratitude for the privilege of working in an industry that I love and respect. Although I have seen the overlooking of human dignity and a number of civil rights and liberties, the increase in acts of violence in recordings and videos, and the contempt for women by some artists, I have been to a certain degree, treated with affectionate friendship from so many. It has not been easy trying to persuade radio station owners and record company executives to believe in the fundamental principles of social and racial equality, and I never felt comfortable attempting to convince them on the subjects of economic and ethical reforms. These are profound and fundamental principles, but I am optimistic that someday the rules of the game will change and the public will have a major impact on local radio programming and the music that is aired will show both tolerance and general acceptance, free of vulgarity and indecency.

Ethical and moral codes in the broadcast industry have been nearly ignored when it relates to cultural identities, particularly people of color. Principled dilemmas have faced minorities for hundreds of years, and in the field of broadcasting, moral values are almost disregarded.

My purpose is not to discredit the broadcast or music business, or those who stand against me or disagree with my views. I do hope that persons who are concerned begin to question the ethical conduct of how the broadcast and recording industry is managed, and how the regulatory agency controls the industries.

It is no secret that mass media influence public opinion and at times, manipulates the truth in advertising and entertainment. Several examinations and varied opinions have been expressed about the art of creative broadcasting, and the early black pioneers through their novel and unique styles, could reach across to the masses. Because of the restrictions of racial bias, racism, Black disc jockeys took part in a revolutionary movement that educated, liberated and stimulated their listeners and their community. These originals achieved a series of "firsts" in their careers, and fought to solve the problems of black unemployment, unfair price increases in African American neighborhoods, and sought equal treatment for all.

I want to express my sincere thanks to those who supported me and have worked tirelessly to see this project completed.

A special thanks to my wife, U.V. and my children and family: Glenn, Cheryl, Sheldon, Lorieann, Patricia, Gina, Elliott, Alfred, William, Monica, Raymond, Harlan, Elgee, Earnest, Michelle and Tanya.

Also, Doris Wesley, Dr. John Wright, Frank Absher.

A sincere thanks and please except my love.

978-0-595-35463-4
0-595-35463-7